Whatever Happened to the Real
Black Country?

BLACK COUNTRY CHRONICLES 1939–1999

Tom Larkin

The History Press

First published 2019

The History Press
97 St George's Place, Cheltenham,
Gloucestershire, GL50 3QB
www.thehistorypress.co.uk

British Library Cataloguing in Publication Data.
A catalogue record for this book is available from the British Library.

ISBN 978 0 7509 9260 2

Typesetting and origination by The History Press
Printed and bound in Great Britain by TJ International Ltd.

Contents

Foreword

You have to take your hat off to Tom Larkin, and other people of his ilk, for taking the trouble to collect and record a myriad of memories and historical facts from not only their own personal life experiences, but also from talking to others who regard their formative years as the good old days. If it wasn't for people like Tom, lots of these aspects of life that many of us have lived through would be lost forever. In this follow-up to *Black Country Chronicles* (2009), he covers the Second World War years in great, and for some nostalgic, detail; examines the post-war era; and explores the dramatic changes that occurred due to technological breakthroughs and a better understanding of health and welfare as the twentieth century gained momentum. The book provides a paddle rather than a brisk swim through the ups and downs of those who were living on the front line of social and economic change, every stroke revealing an aspect of life that is almost unrecognisable to the lives we lead today. But as time marches on every new generation forms its own destiny and comes to its own conclusions about the best way to live life.

It is amazing how the television has completely changed the way we live our lives, in contrast to the immediate post-war generation who enjoyed the wireless in the sitting room, or a regular visit to the local cinema to manifest their main sources of entertainment. This is just one aspect of life we now take for granted that Tom looks at in great detail. At the beginning of the 1950s, just 350,000 households possessed a TV set – one national newspaper at the time made the claim: 'If you let TV through your door, life will never be the same again'. That could easily have been the title of this book, as the box in the corner took control over our lives. The turning point in its popularity was the screening of Queen Elizabeth II's coronation in June 1953, when an estimated 20 million people watched the ceremony. From almost that day on, the television became part of everyday life. It even influenced the style of furniture used in the sitting room and the kind of meals we began to eat.

Tom has compiled a fascinating glance into the last half-century of an era that was dominated by change rather than stability. The details are compelling and make us examine whether life today is better or worse than thirty, forty or fifty years ago. He makes you stop, think and ask the question: 'Were they the good old days? Or are we now living in the world our forebears fought long and hard to achieve for us?'

John Workman
Black Country Bugle

Introduction

This book is a sequel to *Black Country Chronicles*, which ended at the outbreak of the Second World War in September 1939, and continues from that momentous date to depict the history, culture, character and heritage of the area – in particular, its world-renowned workforce, and reputation in manufacturing and engineering until a gradual decline which began in the 1960s. Why or how this catastrophe happened is a matter of continuing argument and debate.

What is beyond dispute is the fact that few of those born in the early part of the twentieth century would have believed that even before the century ended, the region's industrial obituary would have been written.

The memories and experiences collected here were provided by men and women who witnessed industrial, social, and economic change on a scale never experienced before. Events such as the birth of the aeroplane, motor car, wireless, talking pictures, television, plus two world wars and the Great Depression of the 1930s, contributed to a massive transition in people's working and social lives.

Over the period, trade union campaigning was stepped up to establish a shorter working week and improved holiday entitlement. Prior to the passing of the Holidays with Pay Act in 1938, only a third of the workforce qualified for a full week of paid holiday – the new laws made everyone eligible.

Very slowly, the employment situation began to improve from the disastrous low levels of the Depression, along with a rise in quality of life as more and more homes had electricity installed. Before 1936 only 20 per cent of households were connected, this reached 60 per cent by 1938, and created jobs in cable laying, power station construction and power line installation. There was also a surge in car ownership and an expansion in the region's road haulage industry: a great boost to the numerous local firms producing vehicles.

All the signs of economic recovery were, however, increasingly threatened by a growing European crisis originating with Adolph Hitler's rise to power. From the outset, he had made it clear that he intended to embark on a drive to dominate Europe and to create a greater Germany through a policy of massive expansion.

Toll House, Moxley

Prime Minister Neville Chamberlain decided to pursue a policy of appeasement in response, because he was convinced that Britain was far too weak to fight another war. For the same reason, he embarked on a long program of rearmament.

Chamberlain returned from a vital visit to Munich in 1938 clutching a document signed by Hitler, which pledged he would never go to war against Britain. Consequently, the Prime Minister informed a cheering crowd in Downing Street that it meant peace in our time. This proved to be a false dawn, because in 1939 German troops moved into Czechoslovakia, and in response the British government introduced conscription.

On 1 September 1939, Hitler invaded Poland and two days later, in his familiar sober tone, the Prime Minister revealed the news over the wireless that the country was now at war with Germany.

1

The War

The Beginning

Much has already been documented about the Second World War, but it's important that its enormous impact on civilian daily life is never forgotten.

The first indication of what was to become a 'people's war' came with the government's Emergency Powers (Defence) Act passed in August 1939, giving them the ability to requisition buildings, control prices, introduce rationing, establish the right to imprison people without trial – and to impose severe penalties on anyone found guilty of breaking or ignoring any part of those crucial wartime rules. Undoubtedly, these were some of the most Draconian regulations ever imposed on British citizens; dictating people's eating habits, the clothes they wore and, most severe of all, decreed where they worked and, in many ways, controlled their day to day lives.

Initially, everyone accepted that such laws were needed, and there had already been some indication of what was to come from earlier legislation relating to compulsory identity cards and the issuing of gas masks. But before long, people started to question certain aspects of this strict control. Blackout laws became a cause of disagreement, especially with the alarming increase in road traffic incidents. For example, during an inquest into a fatal accident in the Holloway Bank area of West Bromwich involving a municipal bus, court proceedings included strong comments about inadequate clear vision and the obvious dangers to pedestrians – particularly to the elderly. Also remarked upon were the difficulties of walking at night with no street lighting, and vehicles being restricted to only a pencil beam on headlamps.

Everywhere took on a depressing look of wartime life, with sandbags protecting public buildings and every household required to cover windows and doors with thick black material between sunset and sunrise. People were taught how to use a stirrup pump and water bucket, for dealing with fires on outside buildings such as sheds and outhouses. Large silver-coloured, sausage-shaped barrage balloons started to appear in the sky, suspended from strong wire cables attached to a movable wagon. As part of the blackout regulations, councils painted white lines on lampposts, exposed walls, street trees and footpath kerbs. These markings were important in preventing people from stepping on to the road by mistake, risking collision with passing vehicles. Lighting a cigarette outside was forbidden because it might be seen from the air, but a torch could be used provided a layer of thin brown paper reduced the beam of light.

Because of the alarming increase in accidents and injuries, the government had to do something to ease growing public concern. Eventually the harsh lighting regulations were slightly eased. Nightly wireless listening figures jumped to 25 million, and the number of books issued by libraries rose substantially as people opted to stay indoors. There then followed a seven-month calm that became known as the 'Phoney War', when nothing seemed to be happening and people began to question all the restrictions.

When France fell and troops were evacuated from Dunkirk in 1940, the mood of the nation changed dramatically as the possibility of invasion loomed large. Only a small number of councils had made efforts to increase spending on civilian defence, and concerns were regularly expressed that air-raid precaution facilities in certain Black Country towns appeared to be totally inadequate. For example, the town clerk of Rowley Regis (who also performed the duties of ARP controller) publicly denounced the serious shortages, claiming that in Tividale hardly any worthwhile schemes existed. In Willenhall, the chairman of the ARP committee spoke of widespread apathy, warning that if it continued he intended to resign. Fortunately, the situation regarding local factories was more encouraging, as most firms found little difficulty in organising air-raid precautions from within their own workforce. Evidence of this came from the much-publicised visit by Home Office inspectors to the vast Revo works in Tipton, where management and employees received praise for the efficiency of their well-trained team of 150 firefighters drawn from the ranks of its 2,500 workers.

Increased air-raid warnings meant more nights of disrupted sleep, but people were still required to be at their workplace on time the following morning. Households were issued with shelters comprising six corrugated sections for assembly at the bottom of the garden. After digging a hole 4ft 6in deep, the sheets would be bolted together into a tunnel-shaped structure with a covering of soil placed on the top. Many still recall how cold and wet these shelters were during the winter months, because after a period of time they sank low into the earth and any rain would immediately find its way inside, causing severe dampness. These conditions prompted many to stay indoors during a raid instead, either sheltering in an alcove under the stairs, sitting on freezing cold cellar steps or taking refuge under a heavy wooden kitchen table.

Anderson shelter interior

Indoor Morrison table shelter

Bilston Home Guard, 1942

Families living in tiny back-to-back houses used the nearest purpose-built brick-and-concrete municipal shelters. Erected in areas where most properties had no garden, these quickly became the subject of controversy due to their hard seating, low level of cleanliness and lack of heating, or even a door at the exposed entrance, which created numerous problems in bad weather. Not surprisingly people began to shun them, preferring to risk remaining in their own homes. Schools had their own shelters, fitted with slatted wooden benches. During an air-raid warning, teachers would organise gas mask drills or a sing-song to help distract minds from the reality of the situation.

In 1921, unemployment figures fell to the lowest level since official records began, and to maintain maximum industrial output every bus company requested families to refrain from using buses before 9 a.m. in the morning and 4.30 p.m. in the afternoon, when workers were travelling to and from their workplace. Similar restrictions apply even to this day, although the use of cars has increased and unemployment has risen.

The public were also asked to travel by train only as a last resort, with passengers instructed to make certain the blinds stayed down as a precaution against exposing any glimmer of light. Station names were blacked out to confuse enemy agents, and passengers had to be vigilant on badly lit platforms, making sure that the train was alongside prior to stepping out.

A strict system of petrol rationing was introduced, with only people deemed essential to the needs of the community allowed a priority allocation, while posters appeared with the message to exercise caution when travelling in the dark by 'wearing something white when walking at night'.

In May 1940, groups of part-time militias for men between the ages of 17 and 65 were introduced called Local Defence Volunteers (LDV), later renamed the Home Guard. Their activities entailed a minimum of one evening a week doing general guard duties, plus regular weekend training. Other men in that age group became air-raid precaution wardens (ARP), whose main priority was to maintain blackout laws during an air-raid, while some were enlisted for firefighting duties involving a minimum of 48 hours work weekly. The penalty for not complying with any of these commitments was a £100 fine, or three months' imprisonment.

Conscription was brought in for able-bodied women aged 20–30 to fill the gap in manpower created by men being recruited into the armed forces. They were offered employment in munitions factories, or training as railway porters, bus conductors, telephonists, machine shop operators, street cleaners, delivery van drivers and post office workers. Some opted to join one of the services – either the Auxiliary Territorial Services (ATS), Women's Royal Navy Service (WRNS, nicknamed the Wrens), or the Women's Auxiliary Air Force (WAAF). Others trained as nurses or enlisted in the Women's Land Army (WLA). For young girls conscripted from the green fields of Worcester, Shropshire, Warwickshire or Herefordshire, and directed to work in the Black Country, the polluted environment must have come as a complete shock. They gradually adapted, however, and many married and settled in the region when the war ended.

Strict powers were granted to enable local courts to impose penalties for deliberate absenteeism from critical war production. In Dudley, three men from Tipton, Sedgley and Dudley faced a charge of being deliberately absent from work for 12 hours, and were fined £10 each – a very large sum, considering that for working a 75-hour week a man typically only earned £9. The magistrate commented that he hoped that the verdict of the court would prove an example to discourage this happening again, and that the loss of essential output would not be tolerated, with imprisonment a possible outcome for anyone found guilty of being consistently absent.

At Bilston court, a member of the Home Guard was fined £5 for what was described as 'deliberate malingering' by persistent non-attendance from parade and duties over a period of months. A man from the Greencroft area of the town, employed as an electrical welder at W.G. Allen & Sons in Tipton, was fined a staggering £15 for 'continual lateness from work', estimated at 426 minutes of lost output during December 1941. The accused told the court that this was due to an unreliable bus service between Bilston and Tipton, plus his inability to wake early in the morning.

During 1942 at courts around the Black Country, seven local men were fined £15 each because of their constant lateness from work, with magistrates again highlighting the serious loss of essential war materials involved. In similar fashion at Darlaston Court in 1943, four workmen employed at world-renowned nut and bolt works Guest, Keen & Nettlefolds (GKN) were significantly fined for arriving late for work, while another employee was fined £8 for regular absenteeism. The court dismissed the defendant's claim that this was partly due to trouble in walking because of 'corns on both feet'. At Wednesbury police court, two workmen were committed to prison for two months for a similar offence resulting, it was claimed, in the loss of 206 hours of munitions production. There were also numerous cases of people falling foul of the blackout controls – in one month alone a total of thirty families from Darlaston, Wednesbury, Tipton, Cradley, Bilston and Willenhall found themselves fined the standard 50p imposed for blatant infringement.

One decision people found hard to understand was the policy of evacuating families, especially from the London area, to the Black Country because of the Blitz. They felt this very strange, considering that so many vital local industries would inevitably be major targets in air-raids, as well as the fact that the whole region suffered from an appalling housing problem with huge numbers of Victorian slum properties in every town.

There are accounts of the evacuee's arrivals, and how residents reacted towards them. Two from London were billeted in a house inside Hickman Park, Bilston. Their names were Shepherd and Sipthorpe. A family named Clews were housed in Hadley Road and their two children attended the local Holy Trinity Catholic School. In similar fashion, a family from Dagenham named Ling were accommodated in a small back-to-back house in Tame Street, an area containing some of the most dilapidated properties imaginable. The Ling children became very popular with neighbourhood youngsters. Another example is that of the Tyler family: a mother and daughter who came from East Ham in London and found themselves billeted in Hill Street, Bradley. They arrived with all their belongings in a small suitcase, and the whole of the street rallied round to provide clothes and other essential items.

There were very strict penalties for those refusing to take refugees if the local billeting officer decided they had enough space in their home. The odd incident of hostility did occur, with some people complaining about being given no choice in the matter. For instance, five households in Walsall were fined £50 for refusing to provide accommodation even though they had adequate room.

Propaganda, Rationing and Utility Schemes

Public information became part of the propaganda campaign to bolster public morale and remind people of the need for their cooperation and support. So, when tea, margarine, cooking fat and meat were added to the list of food items on ration, reasons were highlighted to justify the entire rationing policy and the following explanations were given to placate rising concerns:

- Prevention of waste
- It freed more shipping to carry other essential cargo
- Stricter rationing ensured food was divided fairly
- Only by a policy of fixed quotas for every household was this at all possible

Families accepted the aims of fair rationing, even though they were aware of a thriving black market; they consoled themselves with the knowledge that those using it risked prosecution. Occasional accusations were made of extra portions been given to housewives said to be 'well in' with certain shopkeepers. Such incidents were isolated, but even so, constant warnings were issued using cinemas, the wireless and newspapers to underline the stiff penalties regarding rationing laws and any deliberate food wastage.

Everyone over 5 years of age was allocated a buff-coloured ration book that contained coupons to last 52 weeks. Children under 5 had a separate green book, and families were required to register with a local shopkeeper for a period of 12 months.

Some Black Country councils adopted a policy of teaching older schoolchildren how to issue replacement ration books. One such scheme involved girls from Etheridge School, Bilston, being trained to become Ration Book Clerks, distributing them from a small office in the town hall under the supervision of the food officer, Mr Fred Barnett. This work was entirely voluntary yet, amazingly, there was never any shortage of volunteers; yet another of the many ways that schoolchildren contributed to the war effort.

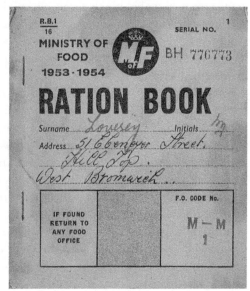

At the beginning of 1941, jam, cheese, sweets, confectionary and canned fruit went on ration – but it was the meagre weekly allocation of tea and sugar that people found the most depressing, because tea in those days was by far the most popular family beverage. On top of that, there was no sugar substitute, apart from the awful-tasting 'saccharin': a tiny white tablet that fizzed and dissolved, leaving a sickly taste in the mouth.

Wartime housewives would stand for hour after hour in queues for specific items – cereals, canned fish and biscuits – available under what was called the points system. These supplies could be obtained at shops on a first-come first-served basis, which meant queuing outside from early morning.

In February 1942, soap was put on ration, and the traditional white bread loaf was replaced with something known as the National Wheatmeal Loaf. Most people found it unpalatable, but accepted its necessity owing to the dramatic decline in imported wheat. That year the buying or selling of new cars was also banned, along with casual driving for pleasure, to save petrol. There was also an advertising crusade with the message of 'frugality in the home' aimed at saving fuel and water. It asked people to turn the lights off in empty rooms, to avoid letting the tap run while washing hands, and there was a special plea not to use more than 5in of water when taking a bath.

More controversy arose over alternative food items such as packets of pure dried eggs, a substitute the government claimed was the equivalent of twelve standard eggs, and dried milk that was simply powder encased in a cylindrical tin, to which water was added to produce a pint of milk. The taste was vile, resulting in it being used in many households only for making puddings and cakes. Housewives developed great skills in devising new ways of utilising the family ration allowance to avoid repetitive meals. They also had to cope with a shortage of all types of bed linen, clothing, household crockery, kitchen utensils, paper, candles and every type of domestic hardware.

Amidst all these hardships, the black market continued to flourish. It was common knowledge that a character known as the local 'spiv' was always around, prepared to supply every type of rationed commodity for the right price.

Ensuring the nation was adequately fed was a constant priority, and the war cabinet decided to make it compulsory for all industries employing a minimum of 250 people to provide canteen facilities. They also launched schemes to establish municipal communal feeding centres, allocating the necessary finances to local councils to convert suitable buildings for that purpose. They were later renamed 'British' or 'Civic' restaurants, to give them more status. Open six days a week (Monday to Friday and until lunchtime on Saturday), they became very popular with factory and office workers, while schoolchildren would also use them on Saturday mornings.

An example of the success of this bold initiative was the decision of Wednesbury council to lease and convert the town's famous Hippodrome in June 1941. Within months of opening, it became a well-used venue catering for an average of 1,200 to 1,300 customers. Another success story came during 1940, when a civic restaurant was established in Tame Street, Bilston, adapting buildings that previously housed a National school (originally erected in 1844 and closely associated with the nearby St Mary's Church). It was also used for various functions such as weddings and social gatherings, and at weekends it would be hired out for ballroom dancing. At one end of this reasonably large, brick-built structure was a huge stage that was used from the beginning of the war for storage of blankets, pillows and bed linen deemed likely to be needed in an emergency.

Undoubtedly, municipal restaurants filled a vital role in providing wholesome meals for workers, and the fact the daily menu was subsidised, providing a typical meal (soup, pork, two veg and a choice of sweets) for as little as 5p, plus a penny for tea or coffee, ensured their continuous success and popularity.

Collecting Household Materials and Weapon Saving Weeks

Everyone was made aware of the need to save things like bones, saucepans, rags, paper and rubber. Parks, gardens and buildings were stripped of their railings to make war weapons, and the Women's Voluntary Service, Boy Scouts, Brownies and Girl Guides all ran weekly street collections. Schoolchildren helped by collecting newspapers, magazines and unwanted books, and councils promoted rivalry between schools to encourage them to reach certain set targets. Those achieving the highest amount would receive a much-coveted certificate.

Wastepaper-saving campaigns were vital to help with the serious shortage of printed material, which had resulted in newspapers such as the local *Express & Star* being reduced to four-page editions. Records show that during 1942 alone, waste paper drives produced an amazing total of 120 tons in Oldbury, 45 tons in Bilston, 75 tons in Brierley Hill, 126 in Dudley, 38 in Darlaston and finally 32 tons in Willenhall.

The government attempted to persuade everyone to save under the slogan 'lend, don't spend', encouraging towns to nominate certain weeks when people would be asked to make extra efforts to reach a new saving target. This involved churches, chapels, shops, factories, public houses, schools and community association groups working together under the supervision of a town committee, and an element of civic pride was introduced to encourage people to get involved, and to donate funds to the war effort.

A typical example of the hard work involved in these special weapons-saving drives happened in Darlaston, where the townspeople were organised to buy ten medium-size tanks at a cost of £150,000. The events began with a parade through the town on Saturday, 15 February 1941. It was led by a unit of the South Staffordshire Regiment, who were followed by a local works band, AFS, members of the Women's Voluntary Service, nursing auxiliaries, ATC, Barrage Balloon units, Boy Scouts and Girl Guides. Along the route, spectators were handed leaflets containing details of forthcoming fundraising events taking place during the week. Included in the varied program was a special municipal-sponsored dance, alongside whist drives, school competitions, raffles, shops, factories, offices and public house collections, talent contests, concerts and an exhibition showing the type of tanks being purchased.

In neighbouring Willenhall, efforts were centred on the purchase of a Spitfire, costing in the region of £6,900. To encourage people to contribute, a captured German Bf 109 Messerschmitt was put on the Wakes ground for public display. On 7 March 1942 they also promoted 'Warship Week' to buy a corvette ship costing £120,000. Overall, the organisation was like that at Darlaston: ending with a gathering at the municipal park, with local dignitaries making passionate appeals for residents to fully support the numerous fundraising events taking place throughout the town.

On 3 April 1943 Bilston and Coseley jointly launched a similar appeal. After marching around Bilston and the town centre of Coseley, voluntary groups and various armed forces assembled for a joint rally in the local park. Residents of both towns were asked to support a full week of activities under the title 'Wings for Victory' to finance an aircraft costing £280,000. Bilston was required to contribute £180,000 and Coseley the reminding £100,000, based on the population size in each authority.

To help achieve that target, saving depots were established in Coseley, Bradley, Moxley, Ettingshall and inside Bilston town hall. The main objective was to persuade people to buy either 2½p, 12½p, or 25p saving stamps. These promotions were a great morale booster, and of great value to the government in its endeavour to control inflation. Information packs were distributed to schools, containing short film clips, booklets and leaflets emphasising how children could help.

Every school held a weekly savings day wherein pupils would be encouraged to save thirty 2½p stamps, which could then be exchanged for a 75p War Savings Certificate that had a guaranteed future value of £1.02½, provided they were not cashed in for a period of 10 years. This government initiative was very successful, and local authorities in co-operation with the National Savings Movement also organised competitions, concerts and open-air talent shows, usually staged on the back of a large touring vehicle at suitable locations.

One such example of this outdoor exhibition took place in Bridge Street, Bilston, with pupils from local schools performing various acts of singing, dancing, poetry readings and gymnastic displays. These performances always attracted a large audience. Their main aim was to persuade people to purchase certificates and saving stamps, and in 1942 a survey revealed that increasing numbers of households were using a portion of their weekly income to support the 'lend, don't spend' campaign, with every working member of the family contributing.

Despite these happy success stories, we must remember that living day to day in a harsh wartime environment had an unsettling effect on schoolchildren. Air-raids meant interrupted sleep and long hours in damp, cold shelters waiting for the all-clear siren. Nevertheless, they were expected to attend school the next day, which inevitably damaged their education – a situation made worse again by the critical shortage of teachers, a result of conscription, creating unavoidable part-time schooling. This meant schools had to cope with the added problem of administering a system of split education, resulting in children attending school on a morning for one week and then afternoons the following week; a necessity which also harmed their learning process.

For some reason, this is a fact of wartime life that has somehow been forgotten. It shouldn't be overlooked – these same children had lived through the poverty and deprivation of the harsh 1930s depression, which makes them an exceptional generation who would later help to rebuild, socially and economically, a nation almost bankrupt from its efforts and sacrifices.

War Years Bring About Wholesale Changes in Lifestyles

Housewives quickly learnt the art of converting old clothes into useful garments and other items for the family, and 1942 saw the start of 'utility clothing' as the government appointed familiar names from the fashion industry to produce a range of cheap but fashionable clothes, with designs under the trademark 'CG41'. These included styles such as men's trousers with no turn up, women's skirts with hems just below the knee, and no frills on suits or dresses.

A shortage of domestic furniture was a persistent problem, because production ceased at the beginning of the war. To help solve this issue, a comprehensive system of 'utility furniture' was introduced; again using well-known firms capable of providing basic types of tables, chairs, wardrobes and other items that were plain, cheap, and serviceable enough that a family could furnish a house at a reasonable cost. This utility policy was later extended to other goods such as kitchen appliances, bed linen and other domestic items. All were subject to government control and production standards, providing a guarantee of high-quality materials and work-manship with strictly regulated selling prices.

Everyone suffered from wartime shortages, but the main burden fell on married women as they struggled to run the home and cope with rationing, whilst working part-time in factories. On special occasions like a social event, family celebration or a wedding, shortages and rationing created even more difficulties – but, somehow, they always seemed to find a solution.

Thriftiness was encouraged by slogans such as the popular 'Make Do and Mend'. Various methods of restoring old clothing were used, with guidelines appearing in weekly magazines that offered tips and instructions on ways to patch up all types of discarded materials and clothes to extend their usefulness. There would be hints on patching shirts and pullovers, and how to make skirts by ripping up pillowcases and sheets before dyeing them, promoted under the government edict, 'What any housewife can do to save buying new'. Advice on making dresses out of old curtains or utilising spare blankets to convert into a coat was also given. Hats went completely out of fashion – particularly among younger women, who began to prefer headscarves. Designers continued to produce clothes with hardly any buttons and a minimum of material, while the number choosing to wear sensible slacks increased substantially.

Despite their many efforts, for most housewives the struggles involved in trying to run the home became more difficult every day, as even small items such as shoelaces, boot polish and household cleaning materials became harder to find. Inevitably there came an acute shortage of soap, lipstick and every other type of cosmetic, so whenever it became known that a local store had received a delivery, long queues would form outside. Because of the serious shortage of stockings, young women would ask a friend or a relative to draw a line down the back of their legs using an eyebrow pencil, which gave the appearance of the real thing. Gravy brown-ing would also be applied to the legs, producing a sandy-coloured look that became known as 'summer liquid stockings'. This was fine providing the rain stayed away, but any sudden downpour would instantly ruin all the painstaking effort.

Acute shortages became a problem for people getting married. The only way of providing a reception was to ask family and friends to each contribute a little from their ration allocation, and most wedding cakes were made from powdered eggs with carrots as a substitute for dried fruit.

Christmas celebrations were particularly frugal by necessity. Poultry was very hard to get and dried fruit for making a Christmas pudding was practically unob-tainable. Other traditional seasonal items were also in short supply, and because most toy manufacturers had switched to producing munitions, there was a scar-city of children's toys, but families did their best to celebrate the season. Most churches had stopped holding midnight services to avoid the difficulties of

Painting on 'summer liquid stockings'

blacking out such large buildings. One of the lasting memories of wartime Christmas occurred in 1942, when the song 'White Christmas' was first heard and went on to become a festive favourite.

Throughout the war, some parts of life continued as normal, as illustrated by this incident at Bilston in 1941. The school medical officer still had to make his yearly report, and commented on finding twenty-five boys and twenty-one girls with unclean bodies, and twenty boys and seventy-five girls having 'hair containing parasites'. He went on to remind parents of their responsibilities and the need to use the new child welfare facilities available at the public clinic.

Despite these occasional reminders of the old every day life, however, shortages continued. That same year, the serious paper shortage forced fish shop owners to request that customers bring their own newspaper wrapping. Then, in 1942, the traditional summer months of June, July, August and September were turned upside down with the introduction of 'double summer time', a revolutionary attempt to maximise food production. During this wartime phenomenon clocks were put forward two hours ahead of GMT, and it would be brilliantly light until midnight, changing the normal pattern of hours of day and night. Obviously, people found adjusting to this new schedule difficult, but they gradually adapted to it. It helped the farming community and provided opportunities for people to work longer on their gardens, allotments and the small patches of spare ground they had converted for growing vegetables to help supplement their meagre weekly rations.

Another impact was the unique sight of people sitting on doorsteps reading the evening paper or a book, relaxing in a chair, or simply chatting to neighbours until very late in the evening. For children it was a playtime bonanza; the extended hours of daylight were an ideal excuse to delay their usual bedtime, while for many adults, sleeping was made very difficult by such unnatural conditions.

In 1943, women became drawn even further into the war effort, when part-time employment for women up to the age of 45 was made compulsory. This new legislation stipulated working for a minimum of 30 hours per week. It also included nursery facilities for mothers with young children for the first time ever.

People began to feel the pressure of these increasing work hours, becoming frustrated over the shortage of leisure activities and entertainment available. In response, many councils decided to allow live shows to be performed on Sunday evenings at local cinemas. These would consist of well-known orchestras, supported by comedy or novelty acts and various types of singers. Meanwhile, ballroom dancing reached a new level of popularity.

Thanks to these local efforts, people could enjoy a good night's entertainment for a very small cost – but a weekend visit to the seaside was virtually out of the question. Travelling became a nightmare because of crowded trains. There was also the additional problem of lack of access to most beaches because of protective barbed wire barriers. To further discourage families from taking seaside holidays, councils organised 'stay at home' weeks: a mixture of municipal dances, town fairs, all types of talent contests, boxing and wrestling shows, plus a mixture of inter-town sports challenges. Meanwhile, thousands continued to flock to cinemas – in 1946 a record breaking 1,650 million admissions were charged in a year in the UK.

The government appealed for young and old to become active in local food-growing schemes in order to make the country as self-sufficient in supplies as possible. Poster campaigns urged everyone to 'dig for victory', 'grow your own food', 'lend a hand on the land', 'wage war on waste' and warned 'don't waste food'. Many people who had never shown the remotest interest in gardening before took up the challenge, and schools started to teach gardening with the use of spare ground allocated to them by local councils. Pupils soon learnt enough about growing food to produce vegetables for distribution amongst the local community.

Many households also turned their back gardens into a suitable area for keeping poultry, pigs, etc. Their methods may have been amateurish, but the end product was worth all the effort. Another success was the collecting of kitchen waste for disposal in municipal pig bins. These would be placed on every street in a weekly cycle. If for some reason a bin was missed, especially during hot summer weather, a foul-smelling aroma would result, and the council department responsible would be inundated with demands for their immediate removal. The local authority was also required to provide facilities that allowed the collected swill to be cooked for a full hour to kill germs and toxins before it become available as pig feed.

Many women became active members of 'forces comfort committees', coming together to knit gloves, scarves, socks and pullovers for members of the armed forces. Many groups later branched out to provide parcels at Christmas. The contribution of voluntary organisations doing this type of work was very valuable. For instance, West Bromwich Rotary ensured that every prisoner of war from that town received a food parcel and knitted comforts. In Willenhall, various sewing groups made dressing gowns and pyjamas for hospital use, and an active crochet circle provided other items.

In every community leaflets and posters began to appear, reminding people that 'careless talk costs lives' and 'walls have ears', indicating a deep concern with the likelihood of foreign agents hanging around, seeking information about factories engaged in war production, and any large movement of troops and materials. Households in the Black Country with German or Italian connections became innocent victims of this mania, and as a precaution they were requested to report to the local police station, to ease public fears.

Beveridge Report Unveiled

The war created great change, but none more so than the Beveridge Report. First unveiled in December 1942, it contained the most revolutionary reforms ever envisaged in relation to people's daily lives. It unleashed a new awareness of the widespread social problems of the past, and provided a blueprint for today's welfare state. It was a plan that would ensure there would be no return to the pre-war levels of unemployment and poverty that thousands of families had experienced.

The author, Sir William Beveridge, and his proposals received massive media coverage in newspapers, and cinemas showed short informational films detailing how people would be affected. The report included a clear definition of five major problems that needed to be eradicated and how this would be financed. These were identified as 'want', caused by frequent high levels of unemployment; 'disease', often originating from the situation of the poor being unable to afford the necessary health care; 'idleness', resulting from lack of work opportunities; 'ignorance' that flourished because of the need for educational reform and the raising of the school leaving age; and finally 'squalor', arising from countless working-class families having no option but to live in appalling slum properties.

The overwhelming public support that ensued reflected years of public pressure by way of demonstrations, petitions, meetings, and debates that had taken place from the mid-thirties for a nationwide welfare scheme. It seems unbelievable that such a plan could be introduced during a war, but Sir William Beveridge would later say in a speech that 'this had been a people's war for a people's peace and my report has become a blueprint for a more just and fairer peacetime for everyone'.

As the war progressed, class barriers became less evident as everyone became committed to the cause of ultimate victory. Not surprisingly, there was also a decline in perceived 'moral standards', as new lifestyles brought about changing attitudes regarding marriage, divorce and sex, plus a significant increase in illegitimacy and broken relationships. There was also a different approach to the perceived role of women in society, and a move to greater emancipation – although the question of equal pay remained a major issue, as employers continued to pay women less than their male counterparts.

From 1942, American forces arrived in the British Isles and soon became a common sight in towns and cities. Dance halls became a magnet for young girls where they hoped to meet American servicemen. Many did, and would go on to become 'GI Brides'.

By 1943, the critical shortage of miners forced the government into selecting by ballot a proportion of male conscripts for vital work in the coal industry. These men were called 'Bevin Boys', named after Ernest Bevin, Minister of Labour.

The need to raise more money to finance the continuing war saw the introduction of a new method of taxation called 'PAYE' (pay as you earn) in April 1944, followed by the all-embracing Education Act, making secondary education up to the age of 15 compulsory.

Sensational Results in Black Country By-Election

Throughout the war, normal political activities were suspended because of an electoral agreement between the Conservative, Labour and Liberal parties. This meant that if any sitting candidate resigned or died, the party that held the seat would nominate a replacement who would be unopposed. This truce did not apply to minority political organisations, however – they were free to contest any by-election. Subsequently, when Mr Ian Hannah, the Member of Parliament for the Bilston/Coseley/Sedgley constituency, died in July 1944 (having won the seat in 1935), it was assumed his nominated successor would be unchallenged.

In this instance the expected formalities could not be followed, because the Independent Labour Party (ILP) decided they would contest the seat, choosing Mr Anthony Eaton as their candidate. This meant a straight fight with the selected National Conservative candidate, Lieutenant Colonel William Gibbons. The election was to be held on Wednesday, 20 September 1944.

Many people believed this to be an unwelcome distraction at a crucial point of the war and an unnecessary waste of precious paper; printing posters and leaflets when there was already a serious shortage. This produced a certain amount of anger about the whole election. Early on in the campaign, the Conservative candidate announced that he had received a personal letter of support from Prime Minister Winston Churchill, direct from Downing Street. Immediately the ILP claimed the letter was a fake and issued a challenge for a public debate on the matter. This offer was declined, and the matter was only resolved when the local *Express & Star* were invited to examine it and determine its origin, which the editor duly did and the dispute ended.

Further controversy broke out when Fenner Brockway, famed journalist and author, agreed to speak on behalf of the ILP candidate. This simply contributed to an already inflamed situation – in 1932, after accepting a previous invitation to visit Bilston, he had made the divisive comment:

Surely no place could have grown up so ugly as this, without some evil mind having deliberately planned to wipe out every trace of beauty.

The statement created a great deal of controversy, resulting in his famous book *Hungry England* being banned by the local council from its libraries and schools, and the author was informed that he would no longer be welcome in the future.

Despite that act of banishment, Brockway did participate, delivering another speech containing descriptions of a similar nature, mainly remembered for one particular passage. He stated: 'In Bilston there are hundreds of houses more suitable for chickens to live in than human beings'. Like his observation of 1932, the speech again proved to be inflammatory, even though a large proportion of the town's population knew many of the comments to be true.

The contest resulted in Lieutenant Colonel Gibbons receiving 9,693 votes, against Mr Eaton's 9,344: a narrow majority of 349. The outcome resulted in Bilston being thrust into the national limelight, with parliament devoting time for a unique post-mortem on its impact. It led to questions being raised as to why so many had decided to support the almost unknown ILP candidate, and most social historians had predicted that the conservative candidate would win easily, mainly because of the war record of Winston Churchill.

Inevitably, when the Labour Party swept to victory in the 1945 election, it surprised many so-called political experts, who had failed to take notice of the message from that famous by-election, which highlighted the fact that people were determined to show they wanted change and there would be no going back to the dreadful pre-war conditions. Change could only be guaranteed by a future government who promised to implement the Beveridge welfare plan.

Final Victory for the Allies

On 6 June 1944, combined Allied forces landed on Normandy beaches – an event forever more to be known as D-Day – and began the long haul to push towards their ultimatum aim to free Europe. Back in Britain, people convinced themselves that this would at long last ensure that the war on the home front was at an end, and they felt safe because it appeared that the threat of further air-raids no longer existed.

Unfortunately, their newfound optimism would be quickly shattered, because in June 1944 the first V1 flying bombs appeared over Britain. These unmanned guided weapons (also known as doodlebugs or buzz bombs) were delivered from sites in Northern France. Their engines made a loud buzzing noise and when this noise stopped there was a brief silence before the V1 dropped and exploded on buildings below. Some of these pilotless weapons were shot down as they crossed the Channel, but large numbers still got through, killing and injuring many civilians and causing extensive damage. They would later be replaced with an even deadlier missile, the V2 rocket. These fearsome rockets were fuelled by alcohol and liquid oxygen, and first appeared over England in September 1944. Hitler believed they would alter the outcome of the war. At the peak of this new style of aerial warfare, around 100 missiles a day were being launched towards selected targets. One of the most horrific examples of the devastation caused was a direct hit by a V1 rocket on the Royal Military Chapel at Wellington Barracks, that killed over 100 and injured many more in June 1944.

The government, ever mindful of the need to maintain morale, decided to restrict information about the cost in lives and injuries. Initially they only published details from West London, with many incidents explained as exploding gas mains to dispel public concern, and removed details about where the rockets had landed. Predictably, this attempt to keep the public in the dark failed, as details of major disasters gradually emerged, plus the grim facts relating to death, casualties and the enormous damage done to buildings. The country's only defence was to rely on anti-aircraft guns and barrage balloons placed along the coast – until in October 1944, when Allied forces captured the launch sites in France, bringing this deadly terror from the skies to a sudden end.

In the spring of 1945, Hitler committed suicide in his Berlin bunker. On 8 May, Germany signed up to the agreed terms of unconditional surrender, and VE (Victory in Europe) Day was declared. People throughout the Black Country took this to be a glimmer of a fresh beginning, and that historical day produced unprecedented scenes of public jubilation. Despite falling rain, neighbours joined together to hold street parties, dancing, games, fireworks and bonfire displays. Special Thanksgiving services were held, while flags, streamers and bunting covered every street and building. Prized family pianos were dragged outside, and stools, chairs and benches commandeered. Somehow, scarce food items suddenly appeared on trestle tables, and whole communities enjoyed the sound of laughter, community singing and a sense of togetherness. Local government buildings and churches were floodlit for the first time since 1939, and every council organised some form of open-air public dancing. Young and old were determined to experience every moment of this memorable occasion, even though there was still the task of defeating Japan.

In June 1945, the government bought in the revolutionary policy of child family allowances, which made provision for the payment of 25p each week – the first indication of future welfare state legislation. The wartime coalition had united the country and there is little doubt that the leader, Winston Churchill, would have preferred to see it continue until the defeat of Japan. Others shared the same hopes, but the majority rank-and-file members of the Labour Party felt an election was long overdue, and voted accordingly at their annual conference. As a result, a general election took place in July 1945, and the outcome was an overall majority of 180 seats for the Labour Party. Subsequently, Clement Attlee replaced Winston Churchill as Prime Minister.

On 6 August 1945, the first atomic bomb was dropped on Hiroshima, followed by the second on the city of Nagasaki on 9 August. This eventually led to Japan surrendering on 14 August. A day of celebration was declared on 15 August, now known as VJ (Victory over Japan) Day, and once again celebrations and expressions of jubilation took place to mark the end of hostilities.

Most people realised that even after achieving peace, they would be called on to make further sacrifices – this time to save the nation from potential bankruptcy. Black Country industries and their workforces would play an essential part in winning what was to be a new struggle: an economic war that would affect the entire country and generations to follow.

2

Cinema

Introduction of Sound

Following the release of *The Jazz Singer*, the first feature-length film with synchronized dialogue, in October 1927, people were no longer content to watch black and white images on a screen with the actor's dialogue written underneath. From then on, silent pictures were destined for the scrapheap, because audiences wanted the new sensation. The financial possibilities soon began to attract businessmen, determined to take advantage of this revolutionary innovation by building luxury cinemas, and the Black Country was quickly identified as a lucrative location for investment.

As the thirties became the undoubted golden age of cinema, these new picture houses were given exotic-sounding names like The Plaza, Alhambra, Imperial, Coliseum, The Regal, Savoy, Picturedome, Odeon, Gaumont and The Tower, and they soon began to dominate every town centre. Famous designers and architects competed against each other to provide the very latest in spectacular interior decoration and lavish design, creating a feeling of sheer luxury with plush comfortable seating, glittering chandeliers, and imposing stairways to posh balconies. A few also possessed the added attraction of an organ to entertain patrons during the interval.

Even though many cinemas were often located within a short distance of each other, they coexisted quite comfortably. Nowhere was this situation better illustrated than in Wolverhampton and its surrounding area, which accommodated fifteen picture houses and two popular theatres, all capable of attracting large audiences six days a week. The brightly illuminated names over every cinema acted like a magnet, and people would queue even in inclement weather until a commissioner, dressed in a military-style uniform and wearing a peaked cap, appeared to announce that there were 'seats now available in all parts'. On Friday and Saturday nights, crowds could be so big that patrons would regularly be greeted with 'sorry, standing room only' notices, but they were content to stand at the back in the hope of obtaining a seat later.

Throughout the thirties, families regarded going to the pictures as a welcome diversion from their day-to-day problems. Even in those harshest of times, it was estimated that 40 per cent of the region's population went to the pictures on average twice a week, because a cinema ticket was relatively cheap and most Black Country management operated a policy of offering reduced admission for unemployed ex-servicemen. Although few working-class families owned a car, there were always cheap bus services available, making it easy for people from smaller adjacent towns to get to larger ones like Wolverhampton, Walsall, Dudley and West Bromwich, or occasionally Birmingham for a wider choice.

Attendance increased even more dramatically with the introduction of split mid-week performances: programmes that ran from Monday to Wednesday, before changing to an entirely different programme on Thursday to Saturday. Each evening there would be a 'first house' starting at 5.30 p.m. and a 'second house' from around 7.45 p.m. There was also the Monday and Thursday afternoon matinee, popular with the elderly.

Every cinema would screen 'trailers' promoting forthcoming attractions to encourage people to return the following week, together with a policy of using cleverly worded slogans to attract maximum audiences, as well as numerous other publicity gimmicks. Evening newspapers would carry a large advertising section, devoted solely to programmes on offer. Advertising hoarding boards located in town centres would display images from various films with the usual message, 'Now showing at your favourite cinema'. Another outlet was to exhibit action extracts from the main film in cinema foyers. Everyone remembers slogans such as 'colossal family entertainment', 'laugh a minute comedy', 'gripping action thriller', 'breath-taking suspense', 'epic western', 'stunning musical' or 'murder, horror and fear' – all corny descriptions, but commercially very effective at the box office.

It's evident to anyone who watches the old black and white films, now shown regularly on afternoon television, that they were mostly mass-produced, with weak storylines, banal dialogue and poor sound. But in those days audiences cared little about quality, they simply wanted to be entertained. More important to them was the opportunity to relax and enjoy the luxury of walking on deep plush carpets, lapping up the colourful décor and enjoying the experience of being escorted to their seat by a smartly dressed usherette.

Cinemas were always a favourite venue for courting couples, often it would be their first date. Quite a number of the less 'posh' cinemas actually provided popular 'double seating' along the back rows. In an era when any outward display of a romantic nature was considered to be 'quite improper', young people welcomed this opportunity for a little privacy.

Inevitably, cinema surpassed the wireless, theatre and gramophone records as the top form of public entertainment. People adopted a routine of attending a cinema and purchasing chocolates, sweets, or packets of cigarettes from the foyer kiosk, while many habitally sat in the same seats every week. Before the programme commenced there would be a babble of continuous chatter, dwindling to a low hush as the brightly coloured safety curtain opened, and a beam of light from the projection window flashed onto the screen. The piercing white light would rapidly cut through the thick blue haze of drifting cigarette and pipe smoke that floated upwards. Later, the cast-iron ashtrays attached to the back of every seat would become overloaded with discarded cigarette ends and matches. During the interval, usherettes paraded up and down the aisles selling ice cream tubs and a selection of soft drinks. On Saturday evenings during the football season, most men would use the break period to take a quick glance at the results in their pink sporting paper, purchased on the way to the cinema, before the lights gradually dimmed and the evening's entertainment resumed.

The motion picture industry opened a whole world of lifestyles and new fashions, with films that depicted many aspects of social and world issues. Inevitably lots of people, particularly the young, started to mimic these trends portrayed by their favourite matinee idols. Weekly journals and tabloid publications such as *Picturegoer*, *Film Pictorial* and *Picture Show*, became very popular. They all followed a certain formula, containing in-depth articles and profiles on individual stars, lots of gossip from the major studios, plus photographs, hints on hairstyles and beauty treatment.

Behaviour on the screen was reflected in people's own daily lives. One example was seeing stars constantly lighting up and discarding cigarette after cigarette, which obviously encouraged smoking. This must seem very strange for anyone growing up alongside today's anti-smoking campaigns. Quirks and styles associated with certain movie stars became very fashionable, such as the long white scarves often worn by George Raft and the trendy moustaches favoured by Clark Gable and Ronald Colman. Slacks or trousers worn by Barbara Stanwyck and other female idols also became quite a craze, so much so that in the early 1940s sales of these items reached a record level. Bette Davis, an enormously admired matinee idol, made the cigarette holder very popular by using one in her films.

One of the greatest instances of screen mimicry occurred during the war, with Veronica Lakes' debut in a run-of-the-mill murder mystery called *The Glass Key*, in which she displayed a controversial 'peek-a-boo' hairstyle that dropped her hair over one side of her face. It was soon widely adopted by girls working in factories on vital production lines. When a safety concern emerged about the danger of loose hair getting entangled in machinery, the government was forced to take action by launching a campaign under the slogan 'cover your hair for safety'. This required machine operatives to wear a protective head square or turban, a fashion that soon became a feature of wartime life.

Veronica Lake

It wasn't the first time that concerns had been expressed about the type of images projected in films. For example, in a court case that took place in April 1937, an 11-year-old boy from Wednesbury was fined 50p for possessing an air rifle without the required licence. During the proceedings, a representative from the local education department submitted evidence that the defendant attended the cinema twice a week, something that they thought should be considered because certain types of violent films contributed to his obsession with guns. Few people would have attached much credibility to these comments – on the contrary, most would have expressed the view that, overall, what was shown in local cinemas was harmless. Every film was subject to the most rigid censorship and anything controversial was given an X certificate, which at the time meant juveniles were not allowed entrance into a picture house unless accompanied by an older person. In one year alone, 300 films were rejected by the British Board of Censors because of concerns about their contents.

The thirties era provided several memorable classic pictures. In 1937, audiences were enthralled by the first ever full-length Disney colour animation, *Snow White and the Seven Dwarfs*, and in 1938 the film *Sixty Glorious Years*, a biography of Queen Victoria, became popular locally because the star, British actress Anna Neagle, made a special visit to Stewarts & Lloyds steelworks in Bilston.

Two further cinematic milestones emerged in 1939. *Gone with the Wind*, one of the longest films ever made, was released and won no less than eight Academy Awards. The other was the fantasy musical *The Wizard of Oz*, which broke new ground by being shot partly in black and white but mainly in colour. Even today, both pre-war classics are shown regularly on television at Christmas or Easter time.

Wherever *Gone with the Wind* was to be screened, cinema management ensured a spectacular display would take place for a whole week beforehand. They also introduced a unique one-off patron's pass, which provided customers with the opportunity to slip out to a nearby public house for a quick drink during the long interval, before returning for the second half of the then-record 219-minute film.

As autumn approached in 1939, and the prospect of war loomed ever closer, cinemas began to include in their weekly programmes short official government information film clips, containing useful tips on air-raid precautions, civil defence and various hints on maintaining the home during wartime. Throughout the immediate post-war period, people's lives were affected by bleak austerity often worse than they experienced during the conflict, with continuing shortages, rationing and widespread controls. Just as they had done throughout the 1930s' Great Depression, families turned to the cinema to obtain some light relief. In 1948, attendances topped the 16 million mark and 'house full' signs became a familiar sight, week after week, outside most picture houses.

Local people often reminisce about the cinema they went to on a regular basis, and among those best remembered are:

Bilston	Odeon, Savoy and Alhambra
Bradley	The Forum
Coseley	The Clifton
Cradley	The Majestic
Darlaston	Picturedome, Olympia and the Regal
Dudley	Plaza, Odeon, Criterion and the Regent
Dudley Port	The Alhambra
Great Bridge	The Palace
Oldbury	The Picture House
Princess End	The Bruce
Quarry Bank	The Coronet
Sedgley	The Clifton
Smethwick	Princess
Tipton	The Regent
Walsall	The Imperial, the Savoy, and the Picture House
Wednesbury	The Gaumont, the Palace and the Rialto
West Bromwich	The Tower and Kings
Willenhall	The Dale Picture House
Wolverhampton	Queens, Odeon, Gaumont, Savoy, Scala, Clifton, the Olympia, the Dunstall, the Rex and the Carlton

The issue of Sunday cinema opening produced great controversy for a long period of time. Petitions were presented to Willenhall, Darlaston and Bilston councils, requesting that cinemas be allowed to show films on the Sabbath day.

These grassroot demands created sharp clashes with members of the then-powerful Lord's Day Observance Society, who were totally opposed to the idea. Nevertheless, after constant pressure, the principle of limited Sunday openings was conceded. It involved a formula of fixed opening hours agreed with local licensing committees, and cinema managers had to agree to make a contribution towards local charities from takings, as well as allowing staff a day off in lieu during the week. They were also required to include government information films on subjects like road safety, public health and cooking hints in their programmes. The first Sunday opening in the Black Country was at the Dale in Willenhall in 1947, followed by the Odeon and Savoy in Bilston in 1949, opening times being 4 p.m. to 10 p.m.

One of the most surprising cinema-going facts concerned people's affection for the many small cinemas located all over the Black Country, known as the local 'fleapits'. They offered patrons a mixture of facilities, including front stalls containing hard wooden benches and an usherette walking down the aisles armed with a spray gun containing insect repellent to deter the fleas. The lighting and decorating in these establishments was crude and minimal. Nevertheless, they are recalled with great nostalgia – especially for amusing incidents that occurred, such as the almost guaranteed break down of the projector in the middle of a film. This would immediately create sustained foot stamping, boos and hand clapping, until the manager appeared on stage to sheepishly apologise and ask everyone to show a little patience, because everything was being done to solve the problem. Such situations were tolerated, mainly because by mid-week money was tight and the nearest fleapit was cheap and convenient, which is why they flourished despite the discomfort. The cheap entrance price also meant there was always a little left over for fish and chips on the way home. Served in yesterday's newspaper, they always had a special flavour that has long since disappeared with the now-compulsory hygienic wrapping paper.

Childhood Cinema Memories

Lots of people remember the Saturday 'crush' at the cinema, which provided an ideal setting for boys and girls to share an exciting atmosphere whilst also using up lots of surplus energy – all for the outlay of a few pennies. It created its own unique environment of yelling, arm-waving and whistling, and always provided the opportunity to consume lots of sweets, biscuits, crisps and all kinds of fruit.

One of the long-suffering usherettes from those days recalled how she dreaded being on duty for the children's matinee, because of the continuous noise. The actions of certain Saturday idols, usually a favourite cowboy, would attract frantic cheers followed by even louder booing whenever the villain appeared – usually dressed in black. The predictable outbreak of fisticuffs between the 'goodie' and the 'baddie' would encourage the usual response of standing on seats to roar support for their hero. A different atmosphere would prevail when the scene switched to a romantic interlude between the hero and the leading lady. Boys especially regarded such interruptions as unnecessary, with comments of 'boring rubbish' promoting prolonged catcalling, until the usual fighting and fisticuffs resumed to wild cheers.

Apart from the western favourites (Ken Maynard, Buck Jones, Gene Autry, Hopalong Cassidy, Roy Rogers, and Clayton Moore as the Lone Ranger, with his trusted partner Tonto played by Jay Silverheels), there were always the comedy shorts featuring such icons as the Three Stooges, the wonderful Laurel and Hardy, Andy Clyde, Leon Errol and Edgar Kennedy. No Saturday matinee, however, would be complete without the obligatory supporting cartoon – either Donald Duck, Mickey Mouse, Goofy or Popeye.

To conclude the afternoon's entertainment, there had to be an all-action weekly serial that always closed with the leading character caught in a life-threatening situation, from which escape seemed impossible. These nail-biting endings were played up by an over-the-top trailer posing the question 'how can our hero possibly get out of this hopeless trap?' followed by the clear reminder to return next week and find out. Without a doubt, serials had a riveting appeal – so much so that certain cinemas added them to their evening programmes, where they attracted a large adult cult following.

Every picture house ran their own Saturday junior club, encouraging youngsters to take up a loyalty card that would be stamped with a star for attendance each week. After obtaining a specified number, the child would qualify for a special gift. There were also club songs to sing along to, such as the one associated with the Odeon cinemas:

Each Saturday afternoon, where do we go?
Getting into mischief? Oh dear, no!
To the Mickey Mouse Club
With our badges on,
Every Saturday at the Odeon!

Being a member entitled children to receive birthday tokens, balloons and regular small packets of sweets. They could also enter a talent contest of singing, dancing or poetry reading, with prizes for the various sections. The old Saturday 'crush' was for many people an important part of their youth, which secures it a place in Black Country social history.

The popularity of cinema continued well into the early fifties, but from 1953 a rapid increase in the sale of televisions brought to an end the post-war bonanza they had enjoyed. Going to the pictures every week was soon replaced by a mania for staying at home to 'watch the box'. Inevitably, this resulted in a drastic reduction in attendance levels, a decline that started a strong fight back by the industry, which invested heavily in more advanced filmmaking techniques, and the conversion of cinemas to accommodate new forms of technology. These costly adaptations were needed for showing 'Cinemascope', 'VisaVision', 'Todd AQ' and the sensational 3D movies such as *House of Wax*, released in 1953, which the makers claimed projected on-screen action directly to patrons. The 3D effect gave the impression of cars, trains and animals virtually leaping out of the screen at people, but the drawback was that they had to wear cardboard spectacles with one red and one green lens to get the full effect. The novelty quickly wore off as the glasses became an irritation, and box office receipts once again began to fall dramatically. Sadly, this led to more cinemas finally closing, with many becoming bingo halls, supermarkets or demolished to make way for car parks. The years from 1959–64 were particularly bad, with the loss of the Picturedome in Darlaston and the Picture House in Willenhall in '59, followed by the Savoy at Bilston in 1962, then the Dale at Willenhall and the Forum at Bradley in 1964.

It's worth remembering that during the war, air-raids destroyed sixty cinemas, but 'going to the pictures' continued to be the most popular form of family entertainment at the time. After the ever-growing impact of television increased closures month after month, the advent of the video proved to be an innovation that would rapidly escalate the problem. Fortunately, this proved to be only a temporary setback: people eventually became bored with television's endless banal programming and, although box office returns remained low, the enterprise of a few film production companies led to the building of large out-of-town multi-screen complexes that brought about a revival in cinema-going. These massive developments are larger, cleaner and smoke-free, with vastly improved acoustics suited to provide for the type of technically advanced films that people crave today. Many traditional cinema-goers claim that these modern picture houses are soulless and have none of the atmosphere of the old days. Even so, they have managed to bring back the appeal of a night out at the pictures – even if some of the old magic had been lost.

3

Childhood Games and Sport

Street Games

Throughout the Black Country, youngsters loved to play their various games. Children used their imagination to organise a variety of activities that provided a sense of challenge and adventure, staving off boredom and idleness. Varying pastimes would herald the arrival of spring, summer, autumn and winter each year, and somehow children had a way of knowing the precise time for changing over from one game to another. They used the relatively traffic-free back streets as a play area, until this became impossible towards the end of the thirties when the number of vehicles on roads increased. This resulted in a number of traditional communal games, once part of growing up in the region, losing their attraction and possibly becoming lost to future generations. Fortunately, there is now a belated, but welcome, acknowledgement that they represented an important part of the region's heritage. As a result, several schools are encouraging their revival as part of recreational activities.

From the beginning of autumn, as the nights slowly closed in, children would meet around an old-style street gaslight, the air filled with the excited noise of boys and girls chatting amongst themselves. Attaching a length of rope to each arm of the lamp post, everyone took turns to swing backwards and forwards. This would go on for hours before their parents arrived to call them indoors. When poor weather intervened, they would gather in each other's houses to play Ludo, snakes and ladders, blow football, draughts, snap or tiddlywinks. They constructed a jigsaw puzzle, or built a crane or bridge using a Meccano set. Some homes had a diamond-shaped 'pitch' board containing numbered hooks fixed at various levels, which would hang from a door. Players would pitch three rubber rings at the hooks to obtain the highest score. Others were fortunate enough to possess a wooden Bagatelle board game, which provided hours of entertainment.

Engrossed in their favourite comics

Another popular pastime was that of buying and exchanging comics, including such titles as the *Dandy, Beano, Knockout, Film Fun, Funny Wonder, Radio Fun* or *Mickey Mouse Weekly*. Sales were huge and very competitive; publishers would regularly offer a free gift that they hoped would persuade youngsters to purchase their publications. There was also the more serious type of comic: *Wizard, Hotspur, Adventure, Boy's Own* and *The Rover*. These contained a mixture of sporting, detective, war, mystery and western stories, depicting the exploits of favourite heroes. Many adults became addicted to the weekly storylines because of the reasonably high standard of writing and, unsurprisingly, various social surveys concluded that they undoubtedly helped to improve standards of reading. Most children would buy a comic to read from cover to cover and then exchange with a friend for a different one. This practice, called 'swopping', provided the opportunity of enjoying a wider selection without any additional expenditure of precious pocket money.

One widespread problem for youngsters was the shortage of recreational facilities during the pre-war and early post-war decades. This arose from the fact that municipal playing fields catering for children were few and far between, especially in deprived slum areas, and red tape regulations and excessive rules made the situation even worse.

Most public parks contained stretches of grass, usually located near carefully nurtured landscapes and showpiece flowerbeds where adults liked to stroll – especially at weekends, often to listen to a local brass band. There were strict by-laws banning all forms of ball games on these areas, rules vigorously enforced by uniformed park-keepers ready to swoop on anyone ignoring the menacing 'ball games forbidden' notices. Because of this, children had little alternative but to play their ball games in back streets, sometimes directly outside people's front doors. This would always lead to confrontation, particularly if the house contained a night-shift worker trying to get some precious daytime sleep. After enduring a succession of balls bouncing off the outside wall, the angry householder would usually shout something like 'Sling your hook and clear off down your own end!' It was useless to protest, and wiser to move on down the street – but after a short time they would receive a similar request to go elsewhere.

The only other option was to find a small piece of industrial ground nearby, which would almost certainly be covered with discarded factory waste, loose bricks and glass. Everyone had to do their bit to help clear the rubbish and create a reasonable playing surface, which, when completed, would become the venue for organised football and cricket challenge matches involving teams from neighbouring streets. These sporting confrontations were taken very seriously, and usually involved a long-standing Black Country tradition known as 'pooling' cricket bats, wickets, footballs and shin pads for the common good of every-one present. Any youngster fortunate enough to own any such equipment was expected to allow their usage to stage these matches, but it was always thought sensible to make that person captain of one of the teams, thereby reducing the possibility that the owner would suddenly decide to go home and bring the game to an abrupt end.

Each of these matches would be fiercely contested, and while they usually began with the regular eleven players, others would inevitably turn up asking to join in, making it quite commonplace for each team to swell to twelve-, thirteen- or even fifteen-a-side. Only the interruption of a heavy downpour or approaching dark-ness would curtail play, otherwise a time limit was never contemplated. When it became impossible to carry on, a diplomatic draw would be agreed, thus saving street pride all around until the next match.

Many can well remember the time when parents were once relaxed about let-ting their children stay out until dark. Until the beginning of the sixties, it was considered quite safe even on dark winter evenings for young girls and boys to attend the local youth club, Girl Guides, Brownies and Boy Scouts, or to visit a friend's house on their own. Nowadays, that has become a rarity. This is a startling contrast to that period when every child grew up in what was perceived as 'danger-free' surroundings, so it's somewhat understandable that senior citizens feel that today's youngsters lose out from not having the freedom they enjoyed. Despite all the daily hardships and poverty in their lives, they still maintain their childhood years were more fulfilled.

At this time, most Black Country children rarely experienced life outside the confines of their local community. Family holidays were virtually non-existent, with even the occasional day trips to the seaside or countryside looked upon as something of a luxury. For many, even the short journey to a neighbouring large town was a rare treat. During the summer break from school, the holiday weeks were used for picnics, camping out, fishing, swimming in the local 'cut, or spending hour after hour over the nearest fields. Anyone owning a tent would be a very popular individual, their friends hoping for an invitation to camp out overnight with them, usually on a bank alongside the canal. This, of course, always required parental permission.

Throughout the long school holidays, groups of children would gather at a prearranged spot early in the morning, prior to wandering over the local fields determined to make the best of a sunny day. They would ensure they had a supply of food and drink enough to satisfy large appetites: jam or lard sandwiches with thickly cut slices of bread, plus an apple or orange washed down with a bottle of cold tea. If a youngster had earned a few pennies running an errand, they would most likely have brought along a bottle of Tizer pop, which would be shared around. As they basked in the sun, comics would be exchanged and the inevitable ball and bat game would commence. Afterwards, bees would be caught in jam jars to be set free later. Other jars would be used to hold the stickleback fish they had caught with a net made from an old stocking.

The beginning of autumn would see a switch to the popular game of kite flying. Children of all ages would wait for ideal windy conditions and then congregate on top of a bank to obtain the maximum amount of lift, before launching their kite into the wind with the aim of reaching a greater height than any others. It required a lot of patience to manoeuvre and control the kite during the upward flight. This was achieved by releasing lengths of twine attached to a wooden spool held tightly in the hand. Hours could be spent on reaching and maintaining maximum height. During autumn weeks, the sky displayed an impressive array of colour that could be seen from miles around. After enjoying these simple pleasures for most of the day, youngsters would slowly make their tired way home, feeling hungry and looking forward to their tea.

There was always a wide choice of things to do and cheap ways of enjoying leisure time. A prime example was that of building a cart by scrounging a wooden crate from a local shop and then stripping an unwanted old pram of its wheels. The roughly assembled contraption would then be carried to a suitable spot with a slight incline, enabling it to be pushed downward to obtain maximum speed. Whoever was in the driving seat steered by pulling hard on a length of rope attached to the front. The only problem was stopping, a manoeuvre that could only be achieved by placing a shoe alongside the wheels and then dragging the sole along as a crude form of braking system. This stopping method was never fully successful. More often than not it ended with the cart crashing to an undignified halt, resulting in a collection of minor bruises and cuts, plus a great deal of wear and tear inflicted upon the shoes. Other popular forms of transportation were foot scooters, which required a youngster to propel themselves along, placing one foot on the iron platform and the other on the ground for propulsion, and there was also always a minority of children with a much-coveted pedal car or an equally desirable three-wheeled bicycle for moving around.

It was popular to indulge in a game of 'Cowboys and Indians' using a replica gun attached to a holster on a belt, with a supply of noisy exploding caps. Those playing the part of the Indians were equipped with a bow and arrow that fired harmless arrows with rubber suckers on the end to avoid any possible injury. Many girls liked skipping, and would often utilise their mother's washing line for this purpose – this would sometimes get them into trouble when mum came to hang the washing out and found the line was dirty. They also enjoyed 'bounce ball', which involved throwing a small rubber ball against a wall and spinning around in a complete circle before catching it on the rebound.

Old style rounders was a favourite of both girls and boys, as was 'pat ball', played with a small wooden bat similar to one used in table tennis. It had a tiny red rubber ball attached to a long length of elastic fixed to the centre, which would be thrown as far away as the elastic would allow and then repeatedly hit hard as it bounced back. Then there was the yo-yo, played by wrapping a length of string around the finger that was attached at one end to a wooden spool. The object of the game was to see how many times it could be spun up and down without stopping.

A popular game among girls was creating 'make believe shops' by collecting empty tins, discarded boxes and cartons. These would be filled with stones to represent items of food. In addition, someone would also bring along their toy post office, tin scales, miniature tea sets, utensils and teddy bears or baby dolls. Dressing up was usually part of this fantasy world, and they would pester mothers or older sisters for cast-off clothes in order to perform concerts amongst themselves in a back yard or courtyard, their imagination knowing no bounds.

Other games such as marbles, conkers, jacks and roller skating were popular, as was bowling a wooden hoop or old car tyre around the back streets, using a wooden stick to guide it along. At regular intervals, races around the block would take place, creating intense local rivalries. Each street would nominate selected runners for each event and chalk lines would be drawn to indicate the start and finish. The races usually consisted of four complete laps around the houses, and arguments often occurred over who had crossed the finishing line first.

Very simple materials could be used to provide hours of entertainment. For instance, the simple activity of making paper aeroplanes by spreading out a sheet of old newspaper and carefully folding the four ends from corner to corner. Bent and shaped until it resembled a replica aeroplane (with a thick front for balance), the plane was then taken into the street, and launched as far as possible into the air, allowing it to glide a considerable distance. The object was for youngsters to compete to see whose aircraft could stay up the longest.

There was also the far more serious form of model aeroplane construction using kits made from balsa wood and propelled by a very strong length of elastic. Later, a company called Airfix produced models made of plastic. It was a craze that often become an obsession: some enthusiasts would happily spend most of their disposable money on this hobby. Many hours were devoted to patient assembling, and ensuring the model matched the real thing as near as possible. When suitable weather arrived, it was taken to a selected spot for its initial flight, an event guaranteed to attract a crowd of onlookers. Sadly, following a brief period of flight, in many instances all the painstaking effort would end in bitter disappointment as the plane crashed to the ground and became a pile of splinters. Such setbacks failed to deter true devotees, who would immediately start to rebuild that same model from the wreckage. Many shared a similar passion for using a Meccano set to make all kinds of things: working cranes, vehicles, bridges and various buildings. This was ideal for those with a flair for engineering; each separate kit could be added to by purchasing various parts from week to week.

Any rain or unsettled weather always provided the ideal opportunity for the indoors hobby of stamp collecting. This required hours of dedicated cataloguing and research. One of the most passionate hobbies of the thirties, however, was that of cigarette card collecting – these would be included in every packet sold and covered numerous topics. Collector's albums became popular for completing sets. It was very lucrative for the tobacco trade, creating a collecting craze amongst children and adults. The coloured cards featured famous people from the world of sport, film, radio and theatre, or a selection of topical subjects and historical events. In 1938, the year before the war, they even issued a set of cards giving instructions on how to safeguard the home during an air-raid, and advice on blackout precautions, air-raid shelters and how to use an incendiary handpump. There were also full sets devoted to plants, railway engines, flags, military badges and tips on gardening and good housekeeping. Children regularly engaged in exchange and bartering sessions, looking for the opportunity to obtain vital missing cards from their albums.

During the spring and summer months, cigarette cards would also be used for playing a game called 'flick card'. Youngsters would take turns standing a certain distance from a street wall, holding a card between their thumb and first finger, before flicking it against the wall. Each player would repeat this action, until a pitcher was successful in getting one to bounce back and cover any of the cards lying on the ground. The winner was then entitled to pick up all the other fallen cards and proceed to throw a card at the wall to start a new game, giving everyone a chance to win them back.

Another popular activity enjoyed by all was 'tick and run', which although physically exhausting, as it required continuous running to avoid being 'ticked', would always provide hours of fun. Far less physical was an activity called 'top and whip'. The top consisted of a piece of wood in the shape of a cone and the whip was a thin stick with a length of string attached. You wound the string around the grooves of the top, then placed it on the ground and pulled the string, causing the top to spin. It could be continually whipped to keep it spinning.

While most childhood amusements were harmless, there were a few that could be dangerous. One was fire can making, an activity in which a tin can would be acquired, and punctured with small holes using a nail and a stone as a hammer. Then it would be filled with small pieces of wood, and tiny particles of coke and coal placed on top. A thin length of wire was attached to each side of the can, threading it through one of the nail holes before bending it into a wide loop for carrying. Finally, a lighted match would be applied to the bits of wood, and as it caught fire the smouldering contents were swung around over the head in a wide arch. The ultimate aim was to find who could create the longest and brightest flame, but on occasions it would result in a youngster receiving a slight burn on the hand or arm after throwing the can as high as possible, creating a shower of sparks as it fell to the ground. This exercise always took place well away from any possible adult observation, ideally on a carefully chosen piece of industrial waste ground.

Equally dangerous was the catapult, made with a small Y-shaped stick and then attaching a strong length of elastic across the front end. A stone was wrapped around the elastic and directed at a chosen target, usually a row of empty tins or a bottle placed on a wall. At times, the window of a greenhouse might be shattered from misdirected shots, leading to a mad scramble to get away. There was also the game of 'Tip Cat' another possible threat to windows. It involved a small piece of wood, sharpened to a point at both ends and placed on to a brick at an angle to the ground. Each player would strike the raised end with a bat, which drove the pointed wood into the air and as it fell it would be given a massive whack. The winner was the person who reached the furthest distance.

As soon as the weather turned cold, various forms of winter recreations came into their own. From the first snowfall, youngsters would bring out their homemade toboggans and take them to a nearby bank for downhill races. The snow would also be compacted to make slides on pathways, which before long would become ice – a dangerous surface, especially outside someone's front door. Whenever this happened, the householder reacted angrily and the children responsible found themselves in trouble.

Inter-street snowball battles were another feature of wintertime, as were efforts to build the biggest and longest-lasting snowman. Any old hat and scarf was uti-lised, along with bits of coal for its eyes and a carrot to make a nose.

On dark winter evenings, someone with a 'magic lantern' might invite friends into their home, where they would watch a collection of moving pictures. This square machine in a box made of tin was capable of showing black and white images projected on to a large white sheet. It was all very primitive compared to the technical gadgets available to modern-day children, but in the thirties and forties it was a thrilling experience.

During this era, a child earning 2½p from running errands or doing the odd job would consider themselves in clover, and lots of thought went into how best to spend it. Should it be on sixteen aniseed balls or five coloured gobstoppers? Or a bag of sherbet sucked through a liquorice straw? There was always a wide choice of penny cakes, too, along with a mixture of cheap broken biscuits. For a small outlay, it was possible to purchase a chocolate bar, plus a selection of toffees and a favourite comic. Whatever the decision, children would always make sure they got the most for their money.

Around the end of October, minds became focused on making plans for bonfire night. Children did extra errands for parents and neighbours, using the money to buy fireworks and various foods such as chestnuts, toffee apples, roasted potatoes, or sausage rolls. Up until the actual day, many hours would be spent on making the obligatory Guy Fawkes effigy. During the week leading up to 5 November, it would be placed in a prominent position in the street and passing pedestrians invited to give a 'penny for the guy', with the proceeds being pooled for use on the big night.

Amazingly, whether in summer or in winter, children had the ability to overcome their often impoverished lives by creating their own ways and methods of enjoying themselves.

Sport

Throughout the Black Country region, sport has always played a significant role in everyday life, providing an escape from the realities of poverty, squalor, and economic gloom – particularly for those returning from both the First and Second World Wars. Football, cricket, boxing, speedway, horse and greyhound racing were the most popular sports, and numerous amateur football and cricket leagues thrived all over the area. Most local industries encouraged their employees to become involved in the works' football, cricket, tennis, bowls or netball teams by providing first-class sporting grounds and many types of equipment. They also funded fishing, cycling and an annual sports day, the latter of which always attracted whole families for a varied day's programme of events, ending with the traditional works' dance in the evening. For many companies, these events were looked upon as a worthwhile public relations

West Bromwich supporters

West Bromwich Albion team

exercise within their local community, creating a valuable sense of loyalty and pride amongst the workforce.

From the early part of the century, towns such as Darlaston, Cradley, Bilston, Lye and Brierley Hill, to name a few, ran their own semi-professional football team. Until well into the fifties, very few families owned a car and most people worked on Saturday, making it difficult to travel very far, so it was the normal practice to go along and support their local town club. A local 'Derby' match could often attract a crowd of up to 2,500 fans.

Inevitably, as increasing numbers of people found themselves able to afford a car, a lot of that regular support fell away as it became easier to make the journey to watch Wolves, Aston Villa, West Bromwich Albion, or Walsall instead.

Football scouts attached to top professional clubs would be present at those local games, looking for potential stars of the future. Up until the sixties, many were discovered in this way, and the four major professional teams in the region always contained players signed from local town teams. This created a close bond with supporters, different from the modern era when so many of the top Premier League sides comprise of players from all over the world.

Although semi-professional teams still attracted a fair amount of support, it was also a fact that most fans preferred watching professional football whatever the inconvenience of getting to grounds. Truly dedicated supporters would travel by bicycle, train, bus or even walk to the Molineux, Villa Park, the Hawthorns, or

Fellows Park. Most weeks, attendances at Wolves, Albion and Villa would average around the 40,000 to 50,000 mark and between 4,000 to 5,000 at Walsall. Most of these stadiums had large areas of uncovered terraces that in the bleak winter months were always cold and windy, the standing sections containing crude concrete crowd control barriers placed a few yards apart. Whenever a goal was scored, the packed spectators would surge forward and back in a manner that was sometimes dangerous and always uncomfortable. No doubt modern day fans find it hard to under-

Three of the Wolves greats: Bert Williams, Jimmy Mullen and Billy Wright

The old Molineux

Wolves 1958-9. Champions for the second year running, with the Championship Cup.
Back row, left to right: Bryn Jones, Eddie Clamp, Bill Slater, Malcolm Finlayson, Eddie Stuart, Ron Flowers, George Showell, Gerry Harris.
Front, Stan Cullis (man), Mickey Lill, Peter Broadbent, Colin Booth, Billy Wright, Jimmy Murray, Bobby Mason, Norman Deeley, Joe Gardiner (trainer)

Wolverhampton Wanderers (Wolves), 1958/59

stand how anyone could endure being crammed in like sardines, making it almost impossible to turn around, but however large the crowd, the turnstiles would only be closed as a last resort. Every ground possessed the most primitive forms of toilet facilities, incapable of coping with huge crowds, and the catering arrangements defied description. The sleek new grounds of today, with their emphasis on comfort, adequate toilet provision and good catering, are a far cry from those awful conditions that were once so common place.

On match days, bus services would be stretched to the limit trying to transport large numbers of people waiting at every bus stop. Those not attending the match would delay going shopping until well after kick-off to avoid that problem. At the beginning of a season, with no floodlights available, all early evening mid-week matches kicked off at 6.15 p.m., which meant there was an inevitable mad dash from the office or factory to get to the grounds on time. Long queues built up at bus stops, and some of the less patient fans would try their luck at waving down passing commercial vehicles to ask drivers for a lift on the back, regardless of the obvious dangers involved.

People sometimes comment on the massive weekly attendance in those days and reflect that footballers were poorly paid at the time, while precious little was spent improving ground facilities. This raises the obvious question of who benefited from those large gate receipts? Certainly not the players or the thousands of long-suffering spectators.

During the pre-war and early post-war years, professional and amateur boxing also enjoyed wide popularity. It was a form of entertainment that was relatively cheap to watch. Tickets for a local match would, on average, cost between 25p and 75p. The success of boxing was reflected in the popularity of publications such as the weekly *Boxing News*, which provided in-depth reporting, pictures and opinions. Fans followed keenly the careers of both top professional champions and amateur stars. This was aptly demonstrated in 1937 by the widespread interest in the heavyweight title fight between Tommy Farr from Wales and reigning world champion, the American Joe Louis. Not surprisingly, the BBC's decision to broadcast the fight live, direct from America in the small hours of the morning, created a sporting sensation – not only because of the disputed result but also the impact on future broadcasting in general. On 26 August 1937, in the early morning, lights in thousands of homes came on as people sacrificed part of a night's sleep to go downstairs, light a fire and make a pot of tea in anticipation of what was then a historic transatlantic landmark.

Before the spread of television, whole families would avidly listen in to wireless coverage of post-war major championship fights. These were presented by the celebrated BBC sports commentator of that era, Raymond Glendenning, assisted by W. Barrington Dalby giving inter-round summaries of contests between a succession of stars that became household names.

Promoters adopted a policy of holding regular contests in places like the Baths Assembly Hall in Dudley, Bilston Drill Hall, the Rink Market in Smethwick, Brierley Hill Town Hall, Willenhall Baths and the Civic Hall in Wolverhampton, as well as other regional venues. Each show would attract large crowds, and the evening's programme always contained a 'needle' contest between two popular local lads. These were semi-professionals who earned their living during the week in a factory or foundry, and welcomed the opportunity to earn a few extra pounds while furthering their boxing ambitions.

Wartime, as one would expect, affected the sporting world. The war brought about a very short interruption to professional football, before it recommenced with the introduction of temporary regional leagues. These enforced changes cut down travelling in line with government transportation restrictions. It was also an acknowledgement that most footballers would be subject to conscription. This made it impossible for the game to function as it had prior to the outbreak of hostilities, so to help overcome the problem a decision was made to allow the use of 'guest players'. The football governing body decided to allow their use on a purely temporary basis. As a result, teams had the opportunity of choosing from a wide selection of conscripted players stationed miles away from their home club ground, so top stars were snapped up to make weekly 'guest appearances'. This system gave supporters from small clubs the chance to watch even established international players performing for their local team.

The wartime structure operated on a regional basis. The area covering the Midlands included small teams like Walsall, Northampton, Crewe Alexander and Port Vale, giving them the chance to compete with their more illustrious and powerful neighbouring clubs. The revised league was not popular with all fans, and subsequently gates dropped to an average of 6,000 to 14,000 attendees, a trend that continued until the game returned to its pre-war structure in 1945/46.

Directly after the war ended, sport in general experienced an enormous boom, and there was also a massive increase in the popularity of football pools. Most households took part in the weekly attempt to win the treble chance by predicting eight score draws. The average stake would be 25p and, amazingly, a survey disclosed that six out of every ten postal orders sold during the football season were placed on the pools. There was also the fondly remembered Saturday teatime routine of families listening intently to the BBC sports report, hoping that the final results meant they had won a treble chance dividend that would change their lives. People of every profession,, from politicians, teachers and lawyers, to doctors and even clergymen, participated.

Specialist newspapers and magazines were available that specifically catered for many forms of sports. For instance, every Saturday during the football season, three evening newspapers were published: the *Sporting Star*, *Sporting Argus* and *Sporting Blue* each provided detailed coverage of Aston Villa, Birmingham City, Wolves,

West Bromwich Albion and Walsall matches, plus action pictures and reports of all the local semi-professional leagues alongside the other sporting results of the day. Racing devotees also had their own journals. The most popular of these was the daily *Sporting Buff*, which cost 2½p, and the 5p weekly *Racing Handicap Book* that contained the latest form, lists of runners, meetings and stable gossip.

Come Saturday teatime there would be the usual scene outside newsagent's shops: crowds awaiting the arrival of the delivery vans, while those going to dance halls, cinemas and theatres purchased their favourite sports paper from a town centre kiosk to read during the interval.

Various indoor games have also long been part of the region's sporting tradition, including snooker, darts, dominoes, cards and billiards. Practically every public house possessed their own team that competed in one of the numerous leagues operating throughout the area for cups and shields. There were also the snooker and billiard halls, many of them located over local Burton Tailors' shops or tucked away in side streets. They flourished in every town, and were always well patronised by large numbers of young men who enjoyed playing snooker on a full-size table, but gambling on the premises was strictly forbidden and it cost 2½p for a thirty-minute session. Predictably, such establishments were subject to criticism and condemnation by religious, educational and civic representatives who considered them to be a harmful influence. It's hard to imagine what their reaction would have been to the high-profile exposure the game of snooker enjoys on television today.

Pigeon flying had a large Black Country following, with numerous pigeon lofts a feature on pre-war estates. Every weekend enthusiastic would be seen walking through streets to the local railway station carrying prized birds in traditional wicker baskets to take part in a race. Bowling, like darts, dominoes and snooker, had a structure of competitive leagues, while throughout the region fishing and club cycling had its share of enthusiasts. Lots of men and women also enjoyed going along to greyhound racing at local venues such as Monmore Green, Wolverhampton, Willenhall Stadium or Perry Barr, Birmingham. For a small entrance fee, people could watch competitive racing, place a bet, and enjoy a drink – particularly popular on Saturday evening. Another popular sport was speedway racing, which during the forties and fifties especially became a popular form of entertainment for whole families, and certain riders became local sporting heroes over the decades.

The greatest boom period for all sports was, without question, the early post-war years. The number of people playing sports virtually trebled, despite the acute shortage of municipal public sports grounds that arose from the failure of local councils to provide enough recreational areas and facilities during the twenties and thirties.

Gambling

Many working-class men and women have long enjoyed a small wager on the Derby and Grand National, but the Street Betting Act of 1906 made betting away from the racecourse illegal. Nevertheless, all over the country betting thrived down back streets, in entryways, alleyways, on concealed patches of waste ground and in certain pubs. The whole business revolved around what were known as 'bookies' runners', who would be paid a fixed commission by a local bookmaker on the number of betting slips taken each day. Around lunchtime they would begin to appear on their familiar patch, or in a discreet corner of a public house – obliging landlords would be aware of their presence but were prepared to turn a blind eye.

Often this routine would be interrupted as policemen, sometimes in disguise, swooped in the middle of transactions. They would even sometimes place a bet themselves to provide evidence at court. Regular raids also took place to apprehend those taking bets at street locations, and there are lots of accounts detailing the ridiculous farce associated with these incidents that often ended in complete chaos. This would happen whenever the bookie's representative had been pre-warned by a neighbourhood resident, who was probably one of his regular clients, fully aware that their betting slip for that day would be confiscated along with all the others by the police. The tip-off allowed the runner enough time for a swift escape over the nearest garden wall or down an alleyway. Whenever an arrest was made, it set in motion a total charade beginning with the formal charge of illegally taking bets in public, followed by the standard ritual of a fine being paid by the bookmaker. This allowed his runner to simply return to the same venue and continue taking bets until the next futile police swoop.

Illegal betting also flourished in factories, and everyone knew the identity of the bookie's representative who accepted bets on the premises. The works' management were usually also alert to the situation, but not unduly bothered provided it never interfered with production.

The 1906 Street Betting Act was viewed with contempt for being unfair, unnecessary and penalising only one section of the community, which is why reforms brought about by the revolutionary Betting and Gaming Act of 1960, which legalised official high street betting shops, was warmly welcomed by all those who enjoyed the occasional flutter. Those controversial restrictions seem so far removed from today, considering the constant pressure from TV and other forms of advertising to encourage people to buy lottery tickets or bet on every type of sporting activity.

This new legislation meant the term 'bookies' runner' disappeared, because under the new laws they could obtain an official document that allowed them to negotiate and receive bets on behalf of a nominated bookmaking agency. These 'betting agency permits' were introduced in 1962, ending a nostalgic part of yesterday's Black Country tradition.

4

Post-War

Changes to Society

By the beginning of 1948, economic prospects began to slowly improve and people started to look forward to an improved lifestyle. Thousands were still living in primitive, unhealthy conditions: 75 per cent of households had no bathroom, while 45 per cent shared outside toilet facilities with other families and 40 per cent of properties were without electricity or gas. The scheme for family allowances (25p for each child after the first born) passed by the wartime coalition helped many families, but the pressure for a better quality of life continued to grow.

In the same year, the government declared 15 July 'a day that would make history', with the introduction of National Insurance via the National Assistance Act and the creation of a revolutionary National Health Service (NHS). This social milestone was the beginning of a long dreamed of, comprehensive welfare state: a description still used today when describing post-war changes to people's daily lives. It was all part of the type of society envisaged by the Beveridge Report of 1942 to give everyone security from 'the cradle to the grave', ending forever all the terrible injustices and hardships of the Great Depression – especially the despised 'means test', a symbol of that poverty-stricken period.

The introduction of the free NHS was arguably the most ambitious policy of social reform ever undertaken by any government, and amazingly it was originally formulated when the outcome of the war was still in the balance. In the pre-war era, most people only called a doctor as a last resort, and visits to a dentist or optician were a rarity. This meant that bad teeth, poor eyesight and all types of minor ailments were a daily fact of life that thousands simply endured because they could not afford to do otherwise.

Under the new act, initially all medical services and prescriptions were free. Dentists, opticians and doctor's surgeries experienced difficulties arising from the large number of people seeking treatment. For a weekly outlay of 24½p, everyone found themselves

Stewarts & Lloyds steelworks, Bilston

Boat built by Rubery Owen, Darlaston

covered for any kind of sickness, works injury or general poor health for the very first time. Predictions of a gradual slackening off in demands for treatment and prescriptions never materialised – on the contrary, it continued to increase.

Then, in 1950, the Korean War began. This forced the government to divert resources from social welfare to finance the war. Reluctantly, a flat rate charge for dental treatment and spectacles was introduced, followed later by a payment of 5p for each prescription that was brought in. It was a decision that led to three major ministerial resignations in protest, and a reminder of changing financial priorities that could threaten the high ideals of completely free treatment. At the same time, the government also had to cope with the problem of increasing industrial and commercial competition from abroad, requiring urgent action to protect certain industries, many of them located in the Black Country. The population also continued to struggle with severe widespread shortages of every description. Regular strikes, together with constant 'go-slow' stoppages that drastically damaged the output of vital exports, meant that even when the Korean War ended, the gloomy economic outlook was slow to recover.

Shortages and the Black Market

The early post-war years saw little respite from austerity and continued rationing. For example, there was a waiting time of twelve months for kettles, cutlery and all types of electrical goods. Clothes rationing in particular was extremely frustrating; men were only allowed one pair of shoes per year and a single pair of socks every six months, while women had to make do with an allocation of one dress per year and a pair of new stockings every two months. Cigarettes remained un-rationed, but most shops only sold their limited allocation to their regular customers. Even beer became subject to restricted supplies in many public houses, whilst things like crockery and carpets virtually vanished from high street shops. The only new furniture available was all 'utility' design, and there was a drastic shortage of razor blades. Every high street and town centre offered the same depressing sight, their shops half empty due to most manufactured goods being allocated for export to solve the crippling balance of payments debt. For most people, the situation only became more frustrating with the activities of black market 'spivs', who were always looking to sell rationed items to clients for profit. Anyone with the necessary cash could use it as a way of getting around rationing.

By the end of 1945, special trains had begun transporting evacuees from the Black Country back to their original towns and cities, but a small number chose to settle elsewhere in the region, mainly because of the employment opportunities. Meanwhile, demobilised servicemen returned to find things completely different to how they had been when they left – and, perhaps, how they had imagined things would be on their triumphant return. Their biggest problem was finding somewhere to live, particularly as a large proportion of homes were in urgent need of major repair. A programme of slum clearance had begun in the thirties, but this had come to an abrupt halt when war was declared. There was also an urgent need for industries to move from wartime to peacetime production, and so, inevitably, the manufacturing powerhouse of the Black Country and its skilled workforce became a vital factor in producing the crucial manufactured goods that supported the nation in the face of possible economic disaster.

A scarcity of every type of raw material meant that house building had to compete with the need to provide new schools, hospitals, and other social projects from the limited stocks available. Many newly married couples were forced to share accommodation with in-laws and faced waiting years to get a home of their own as the demand for new housing kept growing and growing. To ease the situation, the government launched a scheme to provide revolutionary pre-fabricated dwellings consisting of a concrete raft with a metal frame and factory-made pre-fabricated sections, which could be assembled in just under four hours on a selected site. They proved to be an instant success and councils quickly adopted a rolling programme of building 125,000 homes. Their lifespan was estimated to be no more than ten years, and few could have imagined that a large proportion would still be going strong and remain popular with tenants well into the twenty-first century.

Due to the housing shortage, local housing committees began to introduce strict point schemes that determined the needs of each applicant. This did little to allay the anger of people on long waiting lists, so out of sheer desperation a minority resorted to illegal squatting. They occupied abandoned wartime billets and empty public buildings, even though most had no supply of electricity, water, or other necessities.

Various examples of the poor quality of daily life in the region began to emerge on a regular basis, such as the case of a young couple with two children living in a private rented property in Darlaston, just outside of the town centre. The property consisted of a small attic that had no bathroom facilities, indoor toilet or running water supply, with only candles for lighting. This primitive accommodation cost 27½p per week – quite a high rent in relation to the average wage.

Over in Wednesbury an equally alarming revelation, presented to the council by one of its officers, revealed that because of overcrowding, many parents had adopted the habit of letting young babies sleep alongside them in their bed, with all the obvious dangers that entailed. Most were in Bilston, around the Oxford Street area and adjacent side streets where numerous tiny back-to-back dwellings had been built between 1865 and 1866, mainly to accommodate an enormous influx of industrial workers and their families. Neighbouring larger authorities such as Dudley, Walsall, West Bromwich and Wolverhampton also struggled with similar problems but on a much larger scale. Amazingly, thirteen years later, in November 1957, little had changed. A Birmingham newspaper highlighted the situation in Bilston, describing it as 'a place to pass through as quickly as possible'. This simply disregarded the fact that a cluster of towns existed in the whole region, all with a similar environment of endless smoky chimneys, smog, stagnant canals, cooling towers, unhealthy pollution and row after row of streets containing cramped, overcrowded houses.

The article called for action to clear the slums, reclaim land, commence a much-needed programme of establishing more parks and recreation grounds to improve the environment, and above all embark on an urgent policy to move industries away from residential areas. Local councils made things much worse by adopt-ing bureaucratic regulations, especially the short-sighted tendency of not allowing families any real choice when moving them from slum clearance areas, ignoring wishes to be rehoused as near as possible to their old locality. As a direct conse-quence, long-established communities disappeared.

Every housing authority applied their own strict, unbending rules. New tenants were given a book, reminding them of the need to show respect for next-door neighbours, the importance of maintaining their gardens, not playing loud music at unsocial hours, and that painting the outside of the house was forbidden. Also, sub-letting wasn't allowed, or taking in lodgers without the council's sanction, and the weekly rent was expected to be paid on time. They were also warned of regular visits by a housing welfare officer, who came to check that the property was being looked after. At the end of each tenant's handbook there would be the words, 'do unto others as you would have them do to you'.

Housing would dominate the priorities of successive governments, creating a lot of angry debate on controversial decisions made by many councils – for example, the choice made to commence programmes of high-rise development, mainly to take advantage of larger government subsidies for this type of accommodation. This particular trend resulted in the proportion of traditional housing in the Black Country falling dramatically, and by 1966 the construction of tower blocks would represent a third of all new homes being built. Initially, it was considered the perfect answer to the housing shortage, but before long it became a major contro-versial social issue. Problems emerged such as isolation, noise, vandalism and lack of privacy. Mothers became concerned that they couldn't see their children playing many floors below, lifts failed to work on a regular basis, and there were complaints about rubbish being dumped on stairways. To make matters worse, councils had been told that maintenance costs would be cheaper than for standard housing – a claim which proved to be totally false, because repair bills rocketed out of all pro-portion. Decades later, many local authorities would adopt a policy of demolishing certain blocks, while others would be sold off for private lettings and the remainder modernised and vastly improved.

The unpopular autocratic rules that local housing authorities persisted in applying eventually created a general opinion that they were far too dogmatic and unbending. As a result, a meeting took place in early 1963 in Coseley that would lead to drastic changes in the way social housing was administered. It comprised residents from Coseley and Bilston, intended initially to fight for stricter legislation to tackle the appalling problems from daily uncontrolled industrial pollution. Their demands were subsequently taken up by Robert Edwards MP, and following an extensive campaign of public meetings, raising petitions and holding discussions with health officials, the Control of Pollution Smoke Effluent Bill was passed by Parliament, giving councils increased powers of control.

On 1 April 1966, Coseley and Bilston were forcibly amalgamated to form the enlarged Country Borough of Wolverhampton. In response to these new circumstances, the Coseley and Bilston committee decided to extend their activities to cover the whole new authority and extra people within the extended boundaries. During 1967 they also proposed the establishment of a 'tenant's charter' by introducing a unique document setting out ten clear aims and amalgamating all the existing tenant and resident's groups. Agreement was reached to hold meetings with similar resident federations from other areas, and to lobby MPs and councillors for their support. The major object of the proposals was to call for the allocation of housing to be made more representative by giving tenants greater rights and a say in framing future housing policies, and doing away with unnecessary red tape. After years of frustration and setbacks, the 'tenant's charter' (albeit much amended but nevertheless including aspects of those ten demands) finally obtained government backing in 1992–93. Because it originated in the Black Country, it represented yet another special chapter in the region's long history of community campaigning. This was later acknowledged, and the contribution made by Horace Morris (the Federation's first chairman) was recognised, while an MBE was awarded to its long-serving secretary Ken Gretton as a tribute and reflection of the hard work of everyone involved in the crusade.

Morality, Crime and Punishment

Post-war society still maintained strong opinions regarding marriage, parental control, respect for the elderly, public behaviour, crime and punishment, and lax morals. Advertising was subject to firm censorship, while local licensing boards monitored cinemas and theatres. Any content considered in anyway harmful to public morality would be given a special graded certificate. This barred anyone under the age of 16 from admission to that particular film or show, unless accompanied by an adult.

It remained normal practice for children to assist in helping toward shoring up household finances. No sooner did they leave school than they were expected to start work. Usually this meant finishing school and commencing work the following week, and it was normal in most families that a proportion of their wages would contribute towards the family weekly income.

At that time, young people were not exposed to sales pressure as much as they are today, mainly because they were left with very little disposable income to spend on themselves. Even when they entered the adult working world, their newly acquired position did little to change parent's attitudes towards teenagers. Parental discipline could be very rigid; often strict rules would be applied regarding returning home from a party, dance, cinema or theatre at a set hour, and these time limits were always harder for girls in a family. Many can recall missing the end of a film or theatre show to ensure catching the bus home on time. Even when they reached the magic milestone age of 21 and became a fully-fledged adult, if they still lived under their parent's roof certain house rules continued to apply.

Older people are often scathing about what they regard as low standards of behaviour amongst the young, a cycle that repeats by generation. Children had always been taught a code of respect towards their elders and neighbours and some feel that successive governments have abandoned the firm disciplined environment they grew up with, creating many of the present-day problems in society.

Coldest Winter and Hottest Summer

When the war ended people reluctantly accepted that food rationing would continue for some time to come, but throughout 1946 a worldwide food shortage forced the government to adopt a policy of harsher rationing – even bread, which had never been controlled in the war, became subject to rationing until 1948.

On New Year's Day 1947, Britain's coal-mining industry was nationalised and from 23 January snow began to fall heavily. Temperatures plummeted rapidly, gale force winds created 15ft-high snowdrifts, canals froze, and train, bus and road transport was disrupted. Before long, essential food items became thin on the ground (even beer supplies were affected!) and BBC radio was temporarily forced off the air because of ice on the transmitters.

The whole population of Great Britain was soon facing the harshest winter on record, and it was destined to go on for three unforgettable months. The entire country was virtually paralysed and from 7 February 1947 matters took a further turn for the worse, with the Ministry of Fuel and Power introducing a severe cut in the amount of electricity supplied to homes and industries.

High snowdrifts

Charabanc buried
in a snowdrift

For some time, experts had given warnings of a possible shortage of coal, but constant requests to increase manpower in the mining industry to avoid that possibility was simply ignored. The government did launch a belated campaign to recruit foreign labour as the situation became increasingly critical, but unfortunately the National Union of Miners refused to have anything to do with the proposal. Eventually, following frantic government pleas for patriotic co-operation, the union withdrew its opposition – but by then it was too late to have any real impact on declining stocks, and as a direct result, further drastic cutbacks in supplies became inevitable. All households were instructed to switch off their electricity between 9 a.m. and 12 noon, and from 2 p.m. through to 4 p.m. in the afternoon. Street lighting was cut to a minimum and most shops and offices resorted to using candles. The penalty for breaking lighting regulations was a fine of £100, or three months in jail.

Most householders relied on an open fire for cooking and heating, so a regular delivery of coal was essential. Even those households lucky enough to possess a gas ring experienced low pressure occasionally, which greater increased boiling time for even a saucepan of water. Not surprisingly, at the slightest hint of a delivery of supplies to a coal merchant's yard people queued for hours in the bleakest weather for what small allowance they could get. The precious cargo would be taken home, with youngsters and adults struggling through deep snowdrifts, using every kind

Canal-boat workers

of contraption, from old prams to rickety, worn-out wheelbarrows. Out of sheer desperation, old furniture, broken tree branches and even garden fences would be chopped up to provide a temporary respite from the cold. Outside toilets and water taps, so vital to thousands with no inside supply, froze solid because of their exposed position in courtyards. People resorted to wearing socks, balaclavas and hats in bed, and piling overcoats and other clothing on top to give some protection from freezing cold bedrooms. Ice would form on the inside of the windows, and stepping on to a freezing linoleum floor to use the chamber pot was a real shock to the body.

The electricity quota to factories and offices was also completely inadequate, resulting in many firms having to operate a reduced working week of two- or three-days' duration, forcing them to temporarily lay off a proportion of their workforce. As the snow continued to fall, many people found themselves reluctantly having to 'sign on' for dole money until the situation improved.

On the roads, buses were fitted with wheel chains. All newspapers were reduced in size. The unyielding ground made it impossible to bury the dead. Petrol supplies dwindled, making delivery of vital food supplies an even greater task. By early March, practically every council found they had few resources left

Steam train belching out smoke

for gritting, while on the railways it became so chaotic that, on 4 March, a train from Wolverhampton took a total of 20 hours to reach its London destination.

Powerful storms and winds stripped buildings and houses of roof tiles, windows were smashed and chimneys damaged. Hoardings were blown down and many properties had their gable ends demolished. All sport was drastically curtailed, and the postponement of more than 140 football matches resulted in the season being extended until 14 June 1947, the longest on record.

Fresh-growing food, buried under a mass of snow, became frost blighted, with farmers unable to dig into the frozen ground, while the already existing frugal meat ration was cut even further. People stood in orderly queues outside shops, lit by candles and other forms of improvised lighting, for the few items available. It says a lot about that generation that the 'never say die' spirit they displayed during the war also helped in getting them through that infamous winter.

Amazingly, after months of bitterly cold weather, the following summer produced sweltering temperatures in June, July and August, averaging around the high eighties and often even higher. As a result, sometimes pressure on water supplies reached near crisis proportions.

Ice cream manufacturers found it impossible to keep up with demand for their products, whilst some vegetables were in short supply as crops fell victim to the hot weather and large quantities of cabbages and tomatoes were damaged by the oppressive heat.

Towards the end of that year, unions launched a campaign highlighting the fact that a weekly wage of £5.25 was the minimum required to sustain an average family, yet take-home pay for most workers was only around £4.25. It was also the year that National Service for young men aged 18 began; that newspapers found themselves restricted to four pages, following an acute shortage of newsprint; and that the meagre weekly milk allowance was cut even further to 2½ pints a week. Meanwhile, a new pen came on the market that did not smudge or require re-filling: this was the ground-breaking Biro. The big downside to the pen, however, was that its price of £2.75 meant that for most people it would remain beyond their financial reach for some time.

Around this period, the fashion market introduced the revolutionary sensation called the 'New Look'. One store sold 700 suits in the style in just over two weeks to women who craved a change from the strict post-war utility clothes regulations.

The exceptional weather also resulted in a devastating loss of industrial output of vital exports, raising fears of a possible economic slump. Because of this concern, an urgent assessment of the nation's workforce became a top priority, and a new employment registration law was rushed through parliament in November 1947.

It required people not employed in export work to report to their local employment exchange centre. This was for redeployment in that vital area of manufacturing output, so essential to industrial post-war recovery. A high-profile campaign was launched, explaining the government's actions and emphasising to everyone the need for their co-operation and support to overcome the country's serious financial situation. After registration, each person would be interviewed by an official who had the power to direct anyone into a job with a company producing exports. Failure to register resulted in a hefty £100 fine or imprisonment; this applied to both men and women of working age. The Minister of Labour, George Isaacs, admitted when introducing the order that hard decisions would be unavoidable when deciding how each person could best be employed in the overall interest of the country, because utilising the whole workforce to its full capacity was essential to the overall interest of the nation.

Environmental Changes

One of the contributing factors to the Black Country's significant change of image and character was the enormous environmental transformations that occurred in the mid-fifties period. These came about because of the appalling pollution that was an ever-present feature of people's daily lives, especially during the winter months, producing a massive health hazard. Without warning, clouds of thick fog would descend, and the atmosphere became blighted; it was almost impossible for

National Service conscripts

anyone to see a foot in front of them when walking. Buses and trains would grind to a halt, town centres were virtually paralysed as everywhere became obscured by thick fog, and the traffic came to a standstill while a strange silence descended all around. These conditions deteriorated rapidly and became worsened by the combination of industrial and domestic smoke hanging in the air. This type of lethal atmosphere had first been officially identified in 1905 and given the description 'smog', a word meaning the coming together of deadly smoke, fog and industrial pollution. The hearth fire, as it roared away giving off its friendly welcoming glow, contributed greatly to the problem. People's clothes, skin and hair would become coated with soot and grimy smoke, while the unpleasant smell would linger for hours. Housewives found the whole situation totally frustrating as residue began covering windowsills, soiling washing hanging out to dry and invading every nook and cranny in the house. People, when venturing outside, usually covered their face with either a handkerchief or a scarf.

Often the smog would continue for days, and for anyone with a history of chest or lung complaints it could be a real health threat. Hospitals and surgeries would be packed out with people, and doctors worked long hours dealing with patients. Such atrocious conditions required mothers to ensure their children were fully wrapped up during winter months when they went to school or out to play. This meant heavy coats, thick gloves and scarves, often handmade. Boys would be clothed in a jumper, balaclava or cap, and short trousers with three-quarter-length socks. Girls had mittens or gloves, and scarves that were pulled up over the nose and mouth to stop the poisonous air getting into their lungs. Some would also wear a hood-type hat, which kept the top half of the body warm, but did very little for their exposed legs. Whenever warning signs of impending smog appeared, the schools closed and pupils were sent home before the unpleasant yellow sulphur mist began to cover the entire landscape. Fortunately, there was far less traffic about in those days, which reduced the possibility of road accidents from poor visibility.

In December 1952, the country experienced the worst smog and fog conditions in living memory. It brought London to a virtual standstill and, after five continuous days, the death toll there alone reached record levels as people experienced breathing and chest problems. Similar circumstances prevailed in the Black Country, with large numbers dying or suffering from serious lung ailments. Public reaction was swift, with a demand for urgent action to prevent any repetition. These protests would lead to the introduction of the Clean Air Act in 1956, and further new laws in 1968, that stipulated what could or couldn't be burnt on domestic fires. They also contained strict rules for controlling industrial waste and relocating industries away from residential dwellings. Smoke-free areas became established, and local councils were required to commence a programme installing modern domestic fires in every clean air zone.

Almost without exception, families relied on an open fire for heating, cooking and washing, and many lived from week to week on a meagre income. Consequently, they burned a cheaper type of coal that created even thicker clouds of dust that increased overall pollution across the region. During 1944, Bilston was chosen to run a pilot scheme that, at the time, was by far the widest ranging survey into problems of uncontrolled pollution. It was carried out under the leadership of Mr Eric Sheldon, Bilston's official salvage officer, and he used specially designed measuring instruments, together with adjustable gauges/dishes, that he placed at carefully selected locations all around the town. Every two days, the deposits of acid, dust, grime and soot would be collected and taken for weighing and close examination. Before long, they learned that acid soot and smoke particles were falling on Bilston at the astonishing rate of 1,400 tonnes per year, which is why the experiment results greatly interested pollution experts. These sensational findings had great significance for every authority throughout the region because their own towns were being similarly affected by industrial fall out.

Aside from the issue of pollution, there was still the long-running problem of housing conditions to contend with. During September 1944, a report in the local *Express & Star* revealed that out of Bilston's housing stock of 7,700 properties, 2,655 had been designated unfit for habitation resulting from long-standing neglect, disrepair, overcrowding and, above all, inadequate sanitary facilities. Nevertheless, from sheer necessity, people lived in these condemned properties. In response, the town's sanitary inspector, Mr Fred Barnet, stated that an urgent building programme was needed to provide a minimum of 4,000 new houses. From that article in the *Express & Star*, it's easy to understand why, even as far back as 1932, Bilston had acquired a reputation for being the 'slum capital of the Black Country'.

5

Things Ain't What They Used to Be

Loss of Traditions

Today, the word 'smog' is rarely heard, along with other terminology that was once part of daily life, such as 'chilblains': a forgotten reminder of bitter winters of the past. Up until the late fifties when the old-style domestic fire began to be replaced, this wintertime ailment created great discomfort for people young and old. It resulted from the fact that domestic fires only heated a small area of a room which meant that on very cold evenings everyone tended to sit as near as possible for extra warmth, getting an inconsistent exposure to the heat. Within a short space of time their legs and feet would invariably develop red marks of inflamed blood vessels, a sure sign of irritating swelling leading to chilblains. The unpleasant tingling sensation and itching would continue for a considerable length of time.

Also fast disappearing is the word 'courting', the traditional practice of a boy and girl walking out before becoming engaged and eventually getting married. Along with this came the ritual of couples collecting items for their 'bottom draw'. This consisted of various types of bed linen, kitchen utensils, cutlery, dishes, towels and teapots, which were mostly donated on birthdays or as Christmas presents. Because courtships often covered several years, these would soon mount up, so they were usually stored in a wooden box or trunk. The engaged couple would spend many hours planning their wedding, deciding on the type of religious ceremony they wanted and the most suitable location for their reception. This also applied to reaching an agreement on putting together the very important guest list, making sure various aunts, uncles and cousins had not been left out – vital for avoiding any family offence. On top of all that would come the thorny question of where the couple would live. Housing was always a problem, particularly after the war. Normally this meant living with in-laws until qualifying for a council house or saving for a deposit to buy a property. Modern relationships prior to marriage are often much shorter and the simpler courtships have gone out of fashion because many couples nowadays choose to just live together. For those that do marry, it is now the accepted practice to make a list of items they would welcome as wedding gifts from relatives and friends alike.

Lifestyles have changed dramatically during the twentieth century, but older residents still maintain that they enjoyed a 'Golden Age' around fifty to sixty years ago. They like talking about 'the good old days' and believe strongly that back then things were 'much different', because there existed a more caring society with a genuine neighbourly attitude towards others. The disadvantage to that thinking, of course, is the tendency to only recollect the good and overlook or ignore the bad circumstances from those decades, such as the harsh living and working conditions, low wages and widespread squalor.

Daily life for the vast majority revolved around maintaining a stifling respectability at all times, strict censorship, restricted pub opening hours, everything and everywhere being closed on a Sunday, few restaurants, no night life entertainment and limited social clubs. For children, their lives were mainly controlled by parents and a society that believed in boundaries of behaviour that were totally ingrained into the accepted dictum 'children should be seen and not heard' either in public or at home. When they left school, they would be expected to start working and become a family earner, but at the same time were discouraged from becoming involved in grown-up issues until reaching the age of 21. Then, and only then, said the rules of the era, would they be considered mature enough to express an opinion on adult affairs or subjects.

Undoubtedly this situation handicapped the younger generation in many ways, and such biased judgement became even more difficult to understand when National Service was introduced in 1947 for all 18-year-old males. This legislation entailed recruitment of that age group for a period of twelve months but in 1948 was increased to eighteen months duration and on average 72,000 were enrolled each year. It eventually led to the outdated view that anyone under the age of 21 was far too naïve and ignorant about life becoming completely indefensible when, at the beginning of the fifties, a new war broke out in Korea. Many of those conscripted were sent to serve in that conflict after only very brief training, while others ended up in various corners of the world, upholding Great Britain's obligations and commitments.

As a direct result, a long overdue change of attitude occurred in society towards young people. This was followed by a minor social revolution, when the word 'teenager' suddenly became popular and the status of that age group increased dramatically. It was terminology that had been part of American daily life for some time because of their increasing level of disposable income, making them a specific target and lucrative source of profit for big business concerns. This trend persuaded companies in Britain to increase their investments in what had become an expanding market, as

Typical fifties teenagers

youngsters started buying more clothes, cosmetics, records and other similar goods. In addition, 'teenagers' became an influential fashion group, opting to wear their own choice of clothes. Many young men preferred Edwardian-style dress and individual haircuts, gaining the nickname 'Teddy Boys', further asserting their identity, while a minority of teens formed gangs that gained a reputation for causing trouble at holiday resorts and certain public houses. Such behaviour was highlighted in the newspapers, but the bad publicity reached new heights with the arrival in England of the American band Bill Haley and His Comets.

The fresh fifties music 'Rock and Roll' received wide media coverage, especially with the release of the film *Rock Around the Clock* in 1956 that capitalised on the growing popularity of the new craze. As a result, sensationalist accounts appeared of unruly behaviour in cinemas, with reports of dancing in the aisles and seats being ripped out, followed later by similar disturbances in dance halls around the country. This simply increased adult criticism and hostility, with demands that local councils take strong action by refusing licences to show the film. There was widespread reaction throughout the Black Country area. The most controversial response occurred at Bilston, with a council proposal of a complete ban on granting permission for any of the town's cinemas, which only survived after opposition against the proposition failed by just two votes. In today's more relaxed society, youngsters perhaps find it difficult to understand such deep divisions, because older teenagers now have the vote and regularly influence public opinion in many ways.

Life was Better Then

People are sometimes inclined to look back on the past through rose-tinted glasses, relishing any opportunity to talk about their sense of loss for things that once were an important part of their lives. These recollections frequently include an environment of low crime, streets patrolled by police, house doors left unlocked because of little fear of being burgled and children able to play outside in safety.

There are many other aspects of life today that make them angry, such as heating bills and the loss of the electric and gas showrooms that once existed in every town, where people obtained help or information without having to wait hours on the phone, which is now the case since privatisation. Also, many would welcome the return of electric and gas local consumer councils, which in the old days contained representatives from local councils who were able to raise complaints on behalf of their residents. Critisism is also voiced about the disappearance of the old town centres, comprising independent retail shops with their charm and character. They dislike the fact that such shops are being virtually wiped out and replaced by supermarkets and chain stores, creating boring, bland uniformity.

Matron in charge of her nurses

Older residents have long deplored the short-sightedness of closing well-used local railway stations and branch lines under the poorly received Beeching plan simply to save money in 1963. Their frustrations and regrets are the same regarding the removal of old-style matrons from hospitals, the continuing closure of historic public houses, the blatant commercialisation in relation to Easter and Christmas, plus the absence of traditional church bells on Sunday mornings. Followers of sport continually express disgust at the high entrance prices to most football and cricket venues. Also, there is anger over the deterioration of formerly close communities, the spread of antisocial behaviour, mindless graffiti, wanton vandalism, violence and bad language: all symptoms of modern life that would not have been tolerated in yesterday's society.

6

Smoking and Lifestyles

Smoking

In the pre-war decades, people's conception of the smoking habit was entirely different to modern-day attitudes. Men tended to be heavy smokers, while women did so mostly at family gatherings such as weddings, Christmas, parties or at other social events. It was customary for all types of ashtrays to be placed around the living room as the habit became increasingly fashionable. A survey in 1928 revealed that Britain was by far the largest smoking nation per head of population in the whole of Europe. This was particularly evident in industrial areas like the Black Country, resulting from the fact that many people slaved away for long hours doing a repetitive boring job in appalling conditions, and they welcomed the opportunity of the ten-minute morning break for a smoke and cup of tea, and likewise during their lunch hour.

Throughout the war, with all the food rationing that people had to endure, the occasional shortages of tobacco and cigarettes would seem a matter of minor importance. On the contrary, it often created friction, with accusations being made from time to time that certain local shops were deliberately concealing their latest delivery under the counter solely for the benefit of favoured customers, while displaying 'sorry, no cigarettes' signs in the shop window. There was also regular criticism of the government's failure to add them to the list of items on ration, which people strongly believed would have helped to curtail the widespread black market for both commodities.

Smoking increased substantially during both world wars, encouraged by the government. Recruiting posters would typically depict soldiers, sailors and airmen smoking either a pipe or a cigarette. Supplies were made cheaply available to every branch of the armed forces, because it was felt smoking acted as a safety valve to ease any feeling of post-battle fatigue, or conversely, by helping to relieve the boredom of waiting around prior to going into action. During the 1920s there was intensive marketing of tobacco and cigarettes, highlighting their social relaxation appeal, and this increased considerably with the introduction of free gifts, mainly aimed at women. Using cleverly worded slogans, a sale war began between manufacturers, with one well-known brand, Craven A, even claiming that smoking their product could enhance the female image and 'never affected the throat at any time'. It became a common policy to utilise the popularity of sporting personalities to sell a brand. A prime example was undoubtedly the hugely popular footballer, Stanley Matthews, pictured on a Craven A poster indicating that he had changed to that brand 'because it provided a smoother and cleaner smoke'. He was not alone, as a selection of other leading sportsmen of the day made similar claims for other manufacturers.

The practice of 'making your own' also became popular. This entailed using a specifically designed small cigarette-making machine, which could be purchased cheaply along with a packet of very thin white cigarette papers and a supply of loose tobacco. A single paper would be placed between two rubber rollers attached to the device, which would then be sprinkled with tobacco, followed by a process of slowly turning the rollers to create the shape of a normal cigarette. Finally, the gummed part of paper would be licked, binding it tight ready for smoking. People would resort to using a self-making machine when money was scarce, because a packet of cigarette papers and some cheap inferior tobacco cost only a few pence, and even though it produced a poor-quality cigarette, it was less costly.

Adverts designed to convey the message that smoking was simply a harmless pleasure became a feature of daily life from the twenties through to the sixties, and during that time little effort was made by successive governments to alert people to the health hazards associated with it. An investigation carried out in the Black Country during the late thirties revealed that 75 per cent of local men smoked heavily. Such statistics could be confirmed on any working day all over the region, especially in the early morning with the familiar sight of workers boarding buses to their respective workplace. On the top deck, where smoking was allowed, there would always be an atmosphere of thick blue smoke, accompanied by the sound of continuous coughing to clear congested lungs. It was regarded as a normal thing to do – at work, in the home, at sporting fixtures, social gatherings and at most committee meetings there was even a tendency to regard non-smokers as being slightly antisocial.

Nowadays, opinions have totally changed. Tobacco adverts in cinemas, newspapers, magazines and on billboards or television have disappeared under new, strict anti-smoking laws, and smokers are now often frowned upon – in particular by former addicts. Undoubtedly, some politicians and business interests found it convenient for a long time to ignore the dangers involved, but over recent years a more enlightened public has become fully aware of the health hazards.

The motion picture industry for decades was accused of churning out films containing scenes of popular matinee idol stars persistently smoking, and therefore

providing unrestricted advertising for tobacco manufacturers. This prompted a specially commissioned study to examine the impact, especially on young people, and
it revealed some surprising results. For instance, over a period of just one hour on
average, twelve or more incidents of prolonged smoking occurred – mostly in 'B'
class movies. These were cheaply made and shown as support for the main feature
film, but they clearly gave the impression that smoking was acceptable.

During the early thirties, a keenly contested promotion involving most of the
well-known cigarette brands broke out as they each launched high-profile schemes,
offering free gifts for anyone collecting a fixed number of coupons which would
be included with their product. They also published catalogues containing details
of items available under the scheme – these obviously varied depending on the
number of coupons needed, and there was a wide selection to choose from: crockery, garden tools, chiming clocks, bed linen, kitchen utensils, clothes and even a
record player in a coloured carrier case with space for eight records. A pair of lady's
non-ladder stockings required 125 coupons and a much-coveted wind-up portable
gramophone could be obtained with 400 coupons. This uncompromising sales
battle suddenly ended by mutual consent between the firms involved during 1935–
36 because of the excessive costs involved. Other companies in future decades
would introduce simi-
lar coupon offers, but
they were far inferior
compared with those
of the thirties.

John Wayne promoting
Camel cigarettes

There was always a wide choice of brands and types of cigarettes available; enough to satisfy every individual preference. Amongst the many names were Wild Woodbine (undoubtedly the working man's favourite), Gold Flake, Kensington, Capstan (Full Strength), Craven A, Players, Senior Service, Du Maurier, Pasha (Turkish Blend), Park Drive, and Churchman's. Many smokers also became attached to a certain make of matches. Either Swan Vesta (advertised as the pipe smoker's match), England's Glory, Bryant & May or a box of Morelands – all of which sold equally well.

Fixed to the wall outside most backstreet corner shops you would find a self-service cigarette machine, which required coins to be inserted for a packet of five cigarettes packaged with two free matches. Many also sold Barrett's imitation children's sweet cigarettes in a yellow packet; the 'cigarettes' had a red mark on the end to give the impression of the real thing, and were a very popular pocket money purchase. Likewise, replica pipes made of liquorice with markings on top of the bowl portraying embers were also available. Youngsters enjoyed mimicking the habits of adults and these novelties gave them the opportunity to do just that and parents saw no harm in it.

During the Christmas season, famous film and theatre stars would appear on billboards or in newspapers and magazines to advertise gift packs containing either 50, 100 or 200 cigarettes of various brands. They would sell them with slogans: 'This is the ideal present for your nearest and dearest at this festive time of the year'. Most of these celebrities themselves smoked; they were happy to allow their names to be used and were no doubt well paid for doing so.

Results of investigations commissioned by the Medical Research Council were published in 1950, identifying smoking as a potential health hazard. However, the anticipated reduction in the numbers of smokers didn't materialise – this was partly because certain influential pressure groups disputed the findings and, of course, the powerful manufacturers challenged the contents at every opportunity. The influence of these manufacturers was illustrated again in 1951, when a proposal to cut shipments of tobacco to allow larger food supplies to be imported that would ease shortages was rejected because of the fear it would lead to a fall in smoking revenue.

Three years on, in February 1954, the then Minister of Health Iain Macleod (a regular smoker himself) convened a meeting to announce that the government now accepted the link between smoking and certain lung and heart diseases, together with many chest complaints. Nevertheless, the whole subject continued to be given a low priority – especially in 1956, when the Chancellor revealed that any drastic reduction in tobacco sales would require an increase of 17.5 per cent on income tax to replace the estimated loss of income. An additional report confirming the link between smoking and certain illnesses had little impact, apart from a small number of smokers switching to filtered cigarettes. This was because they were cheaper, and there was no tobacco in the filter which made them safer. In 1962, the publication of a survey entitled 'Smoking and Health', sanctioned by the Royal College of Physicians, started to change public opinion but it failed to gather momentum. 1964 then saw the launch of the first so-called 'mild brand' cigarettes, which claimed to have a lower tar and nicotine content, and as warnings about the dangers of smoking began to increase, they became quite popular.

Organisations such as Action on Smoking and Health (ASH) and other similar groups made very slow progress, until a strict policy involving a complete ban on smoking in enclosed public places and in the workplace was introduced in 2007. Along with sharp price rises both for tobacco and cigarettes, it led to a significant fall in the number of smokers. Those who lived through 20s and 50s, when smoking was a large part of everyday life, could never have imagined that the present laws banning smoking would become an accepted reality.

Television

At the close of the 1940s, television resumed transmission following its wartime shut down. Only 350,000 households possessed a set, most of them located around the London area. It would be 1949 before the first Midlands TV centre became operative, and even then people's feelings about its arrival were those of widespread indifference.

In 1950 the *Daily Mirror* made the claim 'if you let TV through your door, life will never be the same'. When people try to explain this hostility that existed during those years, they claim that it was a typical distrust of anything new. Many firmly believed television was a temporary novelty and any suggestion that it would eventually replace the cinema was totally derided. A well-known social expert even speculated that 'this invasion of our homes will ultimately upset traditional family life as we know it,' while a very respected magazine speculated that households would need to ration the amount of time devoted to viewing to prevent the neglect of domestic chores and a decline in normal domestic conversation.

During those early days, shops in every high street placed a selection of TVs in their windows to attract potential customers – but another factor related to the lack of enthusiasm for television was undoubtedly the extremely high cost in relation to the average weekly wage of £9 for men and £5 for women. For example, a small 9-inch screen black and white table model with a Bakelite cabinet cost £37.75. An Echo floor-standing console with folding doors plus walnut cabinet was around £74. A Ferguson 17-inch tinted screen television was £78 or a similar size model cost £83, while the price of a TV licence, introduced in 1946 was £2 for a year.

Those who couldn't afford to buy, could rent a set and many households preferred one with a slot meter fitted so that coins could be put in and once a month it would be emptied and, after retaining rental charges, the company collecting agent would give back all additional money to the householder. Lots of families would use this as a convenient method of saving.

Initially television was very unreliable, particularly the 'tube', which was always likely to break down, and people would become frustrated when the repair engineer always seemed to need to remove the faulty TV 'just for a few days' back to the shop. Many local authorities required their tenants to obtain a covering note to prove that an outdoor roof aerial was essential for adequate reception. This was because it was felt a large number clustered together would create an unsightly environment. The alternative was to use a very primitive hooped shaped, indoor aerial which were useless for obtaining a clear picture. Test cards were displayed on sets in homes during the daily closing down period, to give people the opportunity to adjust their picture quality – something that was a regular necessity.

During those pioneering years, there was just one BBC channel (with limited transmission hours) and it was easy to pick out the homes possessing a TV – especially on sunny summer days because, with those early primitive models, the curtains had to be closed to prevent the sun blocking picture visibility. This inspired manufacturers to market a whole range of solutions to prevent this happening. The most popular was a heavy magnifying glass, designed to reduce the impact of sunlight and make the small screen seem larger.

By 1952, television was still far behind the wireless in popularity. One reason for this was the frequency with which many households experienced the frustration of the picture breaking up when traffic passed the house. This nuisance was avoidable if car owners took the trouble to have a special suppressor fitted, thus preventing interference. Most Shell or BP garages would do this free of charge.

There was soon disenchantment with the weekly output of programs, which had become boring and limited, but with no opposition channel to contend with there was little incentive to offer a more varied choice. The single station would open at 7 p.m. on a Sunday with a panel game, followed by a play. Weekdays would consist of three hours' duration, including the usual old black and white film on Monday afternoons and a full hour devoted to children's programmes. Evenings were not much better, offering a repetitive mixture of ballroom dancing, nature documentaries and outside broadcasts from a theatre, circus, museum, or historic building. This would alternate from time to time with tedious discussion panels, current affairs programmes and political forum debates. There was very little for those interested in sport. It was the same formula, week after week, with little variation.

Winston Churchill disliked television, preferring radio for giving interviews, as did the Archbishop of Canterbury and the Earl Marshal of England. Both were initially opposed to permitting cameras inside Westminster Abby for the corona-tion of Elizabeth II in June 1953. They believed it would prove to be intrusive and stressful for the young queen, but in the end it was decided that as many people should see the occasion as possible and so it went ahead.

Already that year interest in television had risen because of the FA Cup Final, but with the screening of the coronation, sales soon reached record levels. It was estimated that 20 million watched the ceremony on their own sets, while millions more without one watched it in a neighbour or relative's home, and from that historic day on television became a dominant part of daily life.

On 5 April 1955, it was announced that Winston Churchill would be retir-ing, but he had already taken the decision to break the monopoly of the BBC by sanctioning the first commercial television channel. For some time, there had been increasing speculation that this was about to happen, which prompted the BBC to introduce a more varied selection of programmes. This new programming started on a December evening in 1954, with the controversial television adaptation of George Orwell's novel *1984*. No sooner had that first episode ended, than the Corporation's switchboard was jammed with irate calls from viewers from all over the country. Various MPs began criticising the BBC for what they considered to be a total lack of sensitivity in failing to warn elderly viewers and people of a nervous disposition about the controversial scenes it contained.

For months after, newspapers, magazines and discussion panels debated this type of entertainment being shown at peak viewing time on a Sunday even-ing. It was certainly a dramatic departure from the normal BBC fare, but other factors contributed to the public outcry, such as a large proportion of the Christian population who held Sunday as the day of special significance. Consequently, projecting scenes of violence into people's living rooms on the Sabbath was bound to invite a strong reaction. Either way, it was merely the opening exchange of a rivalry that would develop between the BBC and the new Independent Television (ITV) channel, which was launched on 22 September 1955 (initially only available in the London area).

The first commercial channel began in the Black Country in March 1956, and people quickly became enthralled by the output of slick, mainly imported American programmes and the novelty of adverts, plus a wide selection of game shows, talent contests and a variety of other programmes. As the amount of daily viewing hours allowed by strict broadcasting laws was gradually increased, people became more addicted to watching television – amazing, considering the initial hostility towards this new form of mass entertainment, how quickly it became a fixture in most homes. It's interesting to note that during this period, a combined radio and television license cost £3, and remained at that level for a further three years before rising to £4 in 1957 – quite different from today's high cost.

As the television craze accelerated, cinemas strived to remain a commercially viable business and their future became increasingly unsure. TV also began to have a growing influence on people's daily lifestyles in a variety of ways. For example, there was a sharp decline in attendance on Sunday evening religious services and a significant reduction in numbers partaking in leisure pursuits such as reading, knitting, painting, dressmaking and night-class courses. In similar fashion, working men's clubs, youth organisations, ballroom dancing classes, debating societies and local history groups all experienced a drastic fall in membership. There also occurred a sharp decline in the practice of conversation between people, involving the tradition of exchanging news about families and details of events in the local community.

Increased television also began to bring about changes in the fifties' living room, with furniture been purchased solely to provide more space for viewing, including specially designed chairs and tables suitable for eating, followed by 'TV meals' requiring minimum preparation and cooking – a real convenience, as a meal for the whole family could be served up in minutes. This change in eating habits was soon exploited by many firms, with TV commercials highlighting the benefits.

Initially, broadcasting regulations had stipulated the period between 6 p.m. and 7 p.m. as a time of shutdown to allow parents to put younger children to bed and for older ones to concentrate on their homework without distraction. When this restriction was abolished in February 1957, the new commercial channel and the BBC quickly moved to utilise that hour for programmes aimed at a young audience, resulting in the tendency for children to spend more of their leisure time in front of the television rather than playing traditional communal games.

By 1958, a survey revealed, more than half of homes in the region possessed a set, and soon after that television replaced the wireless as the most popular form of family home entertainment since such statistics first appeared in 1928.

A second black and white channel opened for the BBC, followed by another landmark – the introduction of colour in 1967. At first people were cool toward this technology, because of the high cost (around £350) well beyond the budget of most households. On top of this, in 1969 a black-and-white license increased to £6 and £11 for colour.

As the sixties progressed, programmes became increasingly part of people's lives by covering events taking place throughout the world, making it possible for householders to witness history being made and watch changes taking place in society from the privacy of their sitting room. When colour television was extended to ITV, it encouraged more and more families to replace their old sets. At the beginning of the seventies the price of a standard colour set amounted to twenty weeks of an average working-class weekly wage. In 1967 a project known as the 'Open University' began using television as a primary recruiting tool. This was a scheme promoted by Prime Minister Harold Wilson, giving people the opportunity to study for university-level qualifications from home.

Throughout the fifties antisocial content, bad language and mindless violence were a rarity on television screens, then from the mid-sixties the situation changed dramatically as programmes began to include controversial dialogue and explicit sex scenes – plus all types of unsociable behaviour, the sort of material that would have been unthinkable a decade earlier. This new formula was defended by producers as simply being a reflection of a more broad-minded society, and gradually the strict censorship was reduced. Topics such as abortion, religion, marriage, divorce and the abolition of the death penalty became commonplace.

More and more, television's ability to shape public attitudes inevitably became the subject of criticism and debate. A viewer's pressure group, 'Clean up TV', headed by former schoolteacher Mary Whitehouse, began to express their concerns. They organised public meetings, lobbied members of parliament and television companies with their objections, complaining about increased violence, bad language, drug use and explicit sex scenes that they believed encouraged antisocial behaviour. For their part, both ITV and the BBC simply repeated their claim of mirroring a changing social climate and the public wanted that reflected on their screens.

In the eighties, a new wave of technical advances began, and the introduction of video recording created an even greater choice for the whole family. In 1982, Channel 4 began transmission, followed by Channel 5 in 1997. The appearance of compact discs came just as households, once again, began to question the poor quality of programmes on TV, resulting in public interest switching to a growing revival of the type of recorded music they enjoyed before watching television on a regular basis. This growing disinterest also created a yearning for their old habit of regular nights out at the cinema, and the film industry quickly moved to take advantage. Large, multi-screen cinemas sprang up, offering patrons 'blockbusting' films, late-night screenings, luxurious surroundings and even Saturday shows for youngsters. Although they couldn't hope to recreate the unique atmosphere of the old-style picture palaces, they did partially revive the habit of going 'to the pictures' as an alternative to staying home in front of the TV.

In the decades since, there has been an explosion of satellite, cable and digital TV, providing numerous channels to once again influence the way families use their leisure time. It's amazing to think that the once-heavily-criticised 'goggle box' has not only become a fixture in living rooms, but that it started a revolutionary social upheaval in people's lives that few could have foreseen, and will no doubt continue to bring about even greater changes with the relentless increase in technology.

Shopping

One of the factors leading to the demise of the Black Country high street is the gradual move away from traditional shopping. Up until the sixties, every town in the region possessed a mixture of independent shops that were a part of people's lives, resulting in shopkeepers and customers establishing a relationship built up over many years. Each shop had its own special atmosphere and character, becoming places where people could exchange news and gossip about the latest events in and around the community. They also believed in the personal touch by treating people as individuals and listening to their problems, opinions, and family news.

It was the common practice for housewives to shop practically every weekday, because most houses lacked even the minimum of adequate food preservation facilities. Prior to embarking on their shopping routine, they first assisted family members in getting organised for work or school, then completed essential household chores before setting out for town on foot or by bus. This took the best part of the morning, struggling from one shop to another with heavy baskets of commodities – consequently, many shops provided a chair for them to rest before moving on. Usually, the day's shopping jaunt entailed a dash up one side of the main street and down the other while somehow finding time for a quick chat with relatives or neighbours encountered on the way.

For those living in appalling Victorian slums shopping was vital, especially for anything perishable, because they had little to no storage space for keeping food cool in the hot summer months. Some dwellings contained a ledge or alcove, usually at the bottom of steps that led into a cellar, which offered a degree of protection for food liable to go off on warm days, while milk would be kept in a bucket of cold water.

The numerous corner shops were always well used, in part because they allowed purchases to be made on the weekly credit system or 'tick', as it was popularly called, but most women preferred to use retailers in the town's high street when finances allowed. Many Black Country towns contained branches of well-known stores such as Maypole Dairies, Home & Colonial, the Co-op, Woolworths, Boots, Marsh & Baxter, Marks & Spencer, and George Mason grocers. There were also top-brand confectioners, bakers, greengrocers, fishmongers, chemists, sweet and toy shops, ironmongers, dressmakers and haberdashers. A few of the larger shops employed their own errand boy, who would deliver groceries to people's front door on a heavy-framed bicycle. Another feature of shopping tradition in the pre-war and early-post-war eras was a thriving selection of superb outdoor and indoor markets that provided a wide selection of essentials and regular bargains.

Even today, many people still yearn for the nostalgic high streets of yesteryear. The lookalike uniformity of modern shopping areas serves as a sharp reminder of just how much of the local character of the Black Country has disappeared, along with other aspects of local heritage that made the region different and special. Sadly, the distinct has been replaced by the bland, with each town containing the same excessive number of betting, charity and coffee shops, banks and building societies. Most of the traditional, independent retailers that still exist find it hard to survive alongside the increasing competition from supermarkets and massive out-of-town shopping precincts. These huge organisations can buy in bulk and have large marketing and advertising backup, which gives them an enormous advantage, making it difficult for small shops to compete against them. They are also a threat to many of the historic markets in the region and, because they sell beer and spirits cheaply, are responsible for long-established local public houses closing at an alarming rate. Small shops also suffer from the actions of councils treating motorists as 'cash cows' by way of ever-increasing parking charges. Car owners are aware they are being continually ripped off when parking either near their work, or most blatantly whenever they decide to shop locally. As a result, they choose to purchase whatever they want for the week from their nearest supermarket, which offers the bonus of free parking – a fact that appeals especially to young families. This undoubtably creates town centres with boarded-up premises and shops holding closing down sales, a depressing situation made worse with the rise of online shopping from the comfort of the home; a trend that continues to grow.

The wholesale loss of our heritage, traditions and history began with the shameful demise of the local industries, followed quickly by the disappearance of close-knit communities and the slow death of unique town centres.

Boundary Changes Battle

In 1959, the government revealed it was contemplating changes to existing local boundaries, a move that would involve the complete destruction of nineteen historic councils and their replacement by enlarged units of local government through amalgamation. The response from residents living in locations such as Darlaston, Tipton and Wednesbury, along with other towns facing extinction, was predictable: they made it clear that it was their wish for things to remain the same, underlining the fact that Black Country communities have always been fiercely proud of their traditions, culture, heritage and character. Consequently, a decision was taken to oppose the plan and utilise every democratic option available to persuade the government that they should reconsider their recommendations.

The first stirrings of this grassroots revolt occurred in the borough of Bilston on 13 June 1961, with the forming of a citizen's defence committee. The inaugural meeting invited people to come along and support positive action against the proposals of the boundary commission, which would end in 'the death of Bilston'. The chairman and three founding members were all well-known dignitaries. They consisted of Dr R. Abbott, a local doctor, Walter Hughes, a Justice of the Peace, F. Collins, a funeral director, and G. Stead, a local businessman. They adopted the slogan 'Bilston for Bilstonians' and launched what was to become the famous 'Fighting Fund'. Posters were distributed, urging people to join in the struggle.

At that time, the town population was around 34,000. A decision was made to organise a mass petition, which surprisingly attracted just over 19,000 signatures, making Bilston front runners in efforts to persuade other small neighbouring authorities for support of a united plan of opposition. This proved to be a successful move, so in July 1961 Willenhall's 'Fight for Freedom Committee' appealed for financial support for its campaign by holding a referendum for the town's 22,000 population, while Wednesfield council commenced organising a similar petition of protest for their residents in August 1961.

From the beginning, the volunteers in Bilston who offered their help realised that one of the priorities would be raising money to sustain the battle, so they set out a programme of whist drives, coffee mornings, jumble sales, raffles, street and pub collections, dances and concerts, in addition to regular leaflet drops and lobbying. They also introduced the novelty of a replica coffin being paraded through the town, asking people to throw in their loose change. It was afterwards placed in

The protest coffin, with kind permission of the *Express & Star*

various shops, displaying the message that Bilston's entire future as an independent council was at stake. Another tactic was the gesture of five representatives from the town's two political parties, meeting to agree on a truce and sharing a platform openly supporting the campaign. One example is that of local fish shops enclosing a leaflet inside customer's orders with a warning: 'If Wolverhampton take over, Bilston will have had its chips'.

In October 1961, a public inquiry began at Wolverhampton to adjudicate on various objections submitted, including alternative schemes from eight of the region's smaller authorities. These were simply brushed aside, and when the lengthy proceedings finally ended it was announced that the overall findings had been accepted with minor modifications, and implementation of the new boundaries would commence on 1 April 1964. But this decision was a setback that only hardened the determination of protestors to carry on in every way possible within the law. The issue that upset them most was the fact that the evidence they had submitted contained figures and information showing that many parts of the recommendations were bizarre and made very little sense. Without doubt, the most ludicrous example highlighted involved the small area of Moxley, which from the end of the war had been jointly administered by Darlaston and Bilston Councils because of its unusual split-site formation that meant it came within the boundaries of both authorities. As usual, these facts were cast aside and the Commission's solution was to dump the entire area into Walsall, a place that hardly anyone from Moxley had any worthwhile affinity with or desire to live under.

For Bilston especially, this was devastating. Moxley had for years been a vital area for allocating families under its slum clearance programme, providing building land for its ever-rising council waiting list. It resulted in the loss of 850 homes to Walsall, built by the borough, plus the cost of providing roads, drainage and public utilities, also a large area of playing fields developed and located there for the benefit of Bilston youngsters. In 1963, Bilston and Wednesbury Borough Councils, along with three of the region's district councils (Darlaston, Willenhall and Sedgley) decided to take their objections to the High Court. The general election in 1964 resulted in a change of government, raising hopes that the entire concept would be reconsidered. On the contrary, the minister Richard Crossman made it clear he intended asking parliament to approve the legislation. He further, and controversially, accused protesters of adopting undemocratic tactics as part of their campaign.

As the struggle continued, it started to attract nationwide media attention. The BBC produced a documentary detailing facts about the battle and an article showing how small authorities in the Black Country were fighting to retain their proud independence. *The Guardian* commented: 'Their success or failure may well set the pattern of local government for the whole of the country.'

To justify their intentions, the government stood by their false doctrine: that amalgamation would provide more efficient administration, and produce better qualified officials and councillors, without becoming remote from the people and deliver improved services at a cheaper cost to every family. In May 1965, the decision on the 1963 appeal against the government's plans was declared invalid by the High Court and the dispute was transferred to Westminster for a history-making debate that would decide the future of the Black Country region forever.

On 2 December 1965, parliament finally approved the infamous West Midland Order Bill. This issue so important to Black Country residents wasn't subjected to a democratic vote but simply rubber-stamped. The tame surrender was a massive let down, but campaigners continued to maintain it was a scheme contrived by ambitious power-hungry politicians and unelected civil servants solely for the purpose of empire building. In the event, no local MP – apart from John Stonehouse, the controversial junior minister from Wednesbury – attempted to give any plausible explanation for the extraordinary no vote decision. Apparently, he had never intended speaking during the debate and made clear that all along it was his intention to abstain from voting. It's therefore impossible to speculate on what motivated other members not to press for a vote. After the all-night session the Bill was nodded through, and 1 April 1966 was chosen as the amended date for implementation of the new authorities: two years later than the government's original timetable of 1 April 1964, which they had announced at the 1961 Wolverhampton inquiry.

On 23 March 1966, a farewell banquet was held in Bilston to mark the sad end of those long-established councils about to be abolished. The theme adopted for the occasion was spelled out under a massive banner: 'Goodbye to 1,000 years of local history.' After that, on Monday, 18 April 1966, the very first meeting of the enlarged Wolverhampton took place in the Civic Hall, followed by the other newly elected authorities at various dates, but all experienced various problems, with feelings still fresh over the whole divisive outcome. Achieving unity was made harder by inevitable disputes about memberships of committees, with persistent accusations of unfair allocation for members from the previous smaller councils. Most of the local Black Country population remained convinced that a combination of ambitious politicians and civil servants had conspired to replace the system of local administration that had successfully served various historic towns for decades, simply to uphold their ridiculous claim that bigger is always better and more efficient. Those fears were vindicated in 1974 with the establishment of a costly new institution of local administration entitled the West Midland County Council. This unwarranted, remote bureaucracy comprising of Birmingham, Coventry, Solihull, Dudley, Walsall, Sandwell and Wolverhampton, with 104 representatives drawn from each of those authorities, did nothing to improve people's lives. Entirely ineffectual, and throughout its existence a huge financial burden to householders, everyone rejoiced when it was finally abolished in March 1986.

Amazingly, in 2017, over fifty years on and in spite of divisions that still linger of that municipal blunder, politicians discussed pushing through similar unpopular proposals – and this time on a much larger scale. This new legislative body is to be created by joining Birmingham, Coventry, Sandwell, Dudley, Walsall, Solihull and Wolverhampton under a new title of 'West Midland Combined Authority' plus periphery councils, for example, Rugby, Telford and Wrekin. All of this has been rubber stamped without any mandate. This extra level of bureaucracy includes the costly post of an elected mayor, who will be given extensive authority to decide policy on issues affecting every household. Whoever obtains that position will administer affairs alongside a cabinet consisting of seven members appointed from each of the amalgamated councils. This just concentrates wider powers in fewer and fewer hands.

These unwanted changes had been approved at private meetings, giving the public little opportunity to express their views at a time when every council faces the choice of where next to make serious cuts in services. For many, it appears to be a backdoor method of initiating a system of regional federal government: something people do not want. Since the late sixties, concerns have been expressed about the increasing decline of the entire area, which raises justified fears that Birmingham, because of its size, will almost certainly dominate any future regional administration. Without a doubt, the majority of politicians favour such a proposal, and it could prove to be the final obituary of the once unique Black Country.

7

The Effect of Post-War Immigration on the Region

When the Second World War ended, the main priority was that of rebuilding the severely damaged economy, brought to near bankruptcy by the massive expense and sacrifices the nation had made. This could only be achieved by adopting a policy of greatly increased exports. It was obvious that a lot would depend on the efforts of Black Country industries and a skilled workforce in repeating the huge contribution they made throughout the war.

One of the major obstacles to attaining a higher level of manufacturing output was the serious labour shortage that threatened any substantial recovery. In direct contrast, most commonwealth countries were experiencing a slump in post-war work opportunities, and it was these circumstances that led to an historical event in June 1948: the arrival at Tilbury Docks of the steamship *Empire Windrush* with more than 500 passengers from the West Indies and Jamaica.

That milestone is now generally acknowledged as the beginning of post-war immigration, which would gradually increase over consecutive decades, with a large percentage arriving in the Black Country region to fill vacancies existing in local industries and health services. Initially, many experienced difficulties adapting to a new lifestyle and environment – incidents of hostility did occur, mainly related to fears that many would be prepared to accept work for lower rates of pay. Thus, some people expressed concerns over future wage bargaining if this happened, and the situation was not helped by a persistent housing crisis.

During 1955, West Bromwich authority advertised for immigrants to apply for vacancies on its buses, mainly as conductors. A strike was called over the appointment of a non-white ticket inspector, but it was eventually resolved. Meanwhile in Wednesbury, a petition opposing the purchase of a house on a new estate by an immigrant family attracted a little publicity; this also faded after they moved in and became active members within the community.

The start of immigration in the 1950s

Fresh race laws slowly changed attitudes as immigration started to ease the labour deficiency problems in industry, hospitals, public transport and various other public bodies. The new laws helped considerably whenever sporadic incidents arose in areas of possible discrimination, such as housing and employment, which is what the legislation was specifically designed to prevent. Sometime later, in 1968, two significant events occurred related to immigration, one of which was to have a massive impact in the Black Country region. At the beginning of that year there was a considerable increase in the number of (predominately Asian) immigrants fleeing persecution in East Africa, prompting the Home Secretary James Callaghan to introduce a new Commonwealth Immigrants Act in February, removing the automatic right of commonwealth citizens with British passports to enter Britain. Then, on 20 April 1968, Enoch Powell, member of the Conservative Shadow Cabinet and MP for Wolverhampton, controversially questioned the whole concept of a workable multicultural Britain and expressed fears about possible future racial conflict. He was subsequently sacked from the Shadow Cabinet by then-Conservative-leader Edward Heath.

Powell's speech created a political storm that divided the nation, with demonstrations, public meetings, marches, massive media reaction and numerous letters for and against in the press. An opinion poll published shortly after the speech showed as many as 70 per cent broadly agreed with some of his views.

In August 1972 Ugandan ruler General Idi Amin decided to expel its Asian population, numbering around 80,000, mostly introduced into East Africa in the nineteenth century. The majority had British passports and, whether in a gesture of support or from a sense of moral obligation, the then Conservative government allowed 30,000 admissions that were dispersed around the country, many settling in the Black Country.

Throughout the seventies, immigration continued, slowly changing the social environment and make-up of local communities in many ways. New arrivals assimilated by opening restaurants in high streets, providing most of the taxi services in towns, and building temples and other centres of religious worship. In addition, many immigrants established shops on local estates: these were usually open all hours, and offered a convenient service for the neighbourhood. Many became strongly involved in their local communities, joining tenants and resident's associations, helping organise church charities, or becoming politically active as MPs, councillors and officials. Plenty have also thrived in various sports, particularly football, cricket, athletics and boxing.

Recently, the whole question of immigration has once again become a matter of public debate, mainly in relation to Britain's continued membership of the European Union. The subject has come under closer scrutiny because of the EU referendum on 23 June 2016. This amounted to the first opportunity the general public had been given to vote directly on the issue since 1975, when the last referendum was held on the controversial and divisive question of EU membership. After a long and acrimonious public exchange of opinions between those who supported continued membership and others who favoured leaving, it all resulted in a close victory for the 'Leave' campaign.

The close result inevitably created bitter divisions throughout the nation, dividing political parties and families. Protracted negotiations with European leaders led to increasing frustration about the constant changing of the actual date and terms of leaving. At the time of writing, the future remains uncertain.

Addendum

Black Country Twentieth-Century Alphabet

Twenty-six letters that relate to an important aspect of twentieth-century Black Country life.

A	Altruism	Willingness of Black Country people to act for the good of others less fortunate in their neighbourhood.
	Austerity	The severe austerity that existed throughout most of a harsh thirties depression and the years immediately after the First and Second World Wars.
B	Betrayal	Broken promises made to returning ex-servicemen, contained in a historic speech by Prime Minister David Lloyd George that he delivered in Wolverhampton on 22 November 1918.
	Boundary changes	Forced amalgamation and loss of independence in the sixties from unwanted changes leading to the disappearance of long-established Black Country councils and the break up of established communities.
C	Cinema	How the coming of talking pictures influenced daily life in so many ways.
	Corner shops	Once a vital part of local community life during the twenties, thirties, forties and early fifties. They sold just about everything imaginable, but most of all provided a system called 'on the tick'. This was a well-used method for households to purchase food and other essential items and pay for them at the end of the week.
D	Depression	The appalling economic slump of the thirties, resulting in abject poverty all over the region and the introduction of the infamous 'means test'.
	Discipline	In the home and in the local community, every child was expected to show respect to adults and obey their parents without question.

E	Education	Mainly provided by county councils and church schools, all of them functioning on policies of firm discipline, respect for teachers and no-nonsense teaching methods.
	Employment	The Black Country was looked upon as the 'nation's manufacturing centre'. Numerous local firms provided employment for generations of families and made available apprenticeships to their children, thus ensuring a continuing skilled workforce for the region.
F	Family life	Chores were shared by every member of the household, with youngsters expected to run errands. Daughters were invariably allocated domestic chores around the house.
	Food	Traditional Black Country dishes include huge fry-ups, bread pudding, pig's feet, rabbit stew, faggots and peas, grey peas, black pudding, chitterlings and klondykes (sliced potato covered in batter).
G	Games (outdoors)	Seasonal street games included playing around gas-lights, tip-cat, cricket, round the houses races, hopscotch, skipping, football, kite flying, fire cans, top and whip, make believe and tea parties with dolls.
	General Strike	First ever national strike occurred in 1926; inevitably a vast majority of Black Country workforce was involved. Predictably, it ended in total failure and many local workers found themselves not being re-employed, a situation that left a legacy of bitterness for decades.
H	Health	Standards were very poor, not helped by overcrowding problems. People were afraid to call a doctor because of the cost. Hospitals relied on voluntary contributions and flag days for support; a situation that lasted until the introduction of free health service in 1948.
	Housing	Large areas of run-down Victorian dwellings existed in every Black Country town well into the sixties. Mainly infamous 'back-to-back' housing, mostly in appalling states of repair. Other similar properties were in small courtyards usually with limited facilities, no indoor water suppl and very primitive toilets outside, etc. These served two, three, four and more families. The majority suffered from leaking roofs, poor drainage and shocking overcrowding.
	Hobbies	Train spotting, model aeroplane construction, stamp collecting, cigarette card collecting, comic swapping.
I	Industry	Internationally known Black Country firms that earned the area recognition as the 'workshop of the world' include: Rubery Owen, Thompsons, Ever Ready, Patent Shaft, the Cannon, GKN – Sankeys, FH Lloyd, Tarmac, Boulton Paul, Sunbeam and many, many others.

J	Jargon (Black Country Slang)	The unique local dialect with particular phases and descriptions which many outside people were unable to understand, such as 'yampy' meaning useless or hopeless, 'baygona' meaning 'I am not going to do it' and 'owbinya' or 'how are you'.
K	Kinship	Close-knit communities, extended families living in the same street or neighbourhood and visiting on a regular basis.
L	Landlords	Absent owners of slum properties who did little to keep their houses in decent repair.
	Leisure	Keeping allotments, gardening, pigeon flying, ballroom dancing, cycling, rambling, ice-skating, amateur dramatics, cinema and swimming.
M	Marriage and courting	It was traditional for young people to go through a period of courting before marriage. They would often create what was known as 'their bottom draw', collecting various items in preparation. Weeks to months were spent on planning the wedding guest list and type of reception, making sure as many close relatives as possible received an invitation to avoid any family offence.
	Means test	A symbol of the thirties' depression created lasting bitter memories throughout the Black Country, especially its intrusion into people's private lives.
N	Neighbourliness	Friendships that developed among neighbours that lasted a lifetime. Readiness to help others in time of need was widespread.
	Nit nurse	The humiliation of being sent home from school following a visit from the 'nit nurse' who had discovered head lice. Then the smelly treatment to be endured getting rid of them – and worse, having large portions of hair cut off.
O	Occupations	Street salesmen who were once a common sight on the Black Country roads, knife grinders, salt sellers, pikelet men, watercress sellers, chimney sweeps, and ice cream bicycle vendors too.
	Outspokenness	True Black Country men and women have always had a reputation for being blunt and direct in their character and forthright with their opinions on most subjects.
	Outdoor toilet and 'brew' house for washing	Outdoor toilets in winter months had limited light and used cut up newspaper squares for toilet paper. Cold unlit 'brew' houses were for washing provision, and had only a primitive lamp or candles for lighting purposes.

P	Pawn shops	Severe poverty forced people to pawn belongings to ensure food was available to feed the family. Even clothing would be taken in on a Monday and retrieved on a Friday. A custom that sadly is still with us today.
	Pollution	From the twenties to the fifties there existed an environment of dirt, smoke, noise, polluted canals and industrial eyesores. Housewives constantly battled to keep their washing free from flying soot and the grime in the atmosphere.
Q	Queues	A regular feature of day to day living during wartime. Housewives had no option other than to queue for hours for food and other essential household items. They continued to do so during the early post-war years, when rationing was retained to cope with massive peacetime shortages. It became an accepted way of life: people would queue at cinemas, theatres, dance halls and sport grounds. Rationing only ended in 1954.
R	Rag and bone man	A regular sight on streets, with children eager to take him a few rags in exchange for a goldfish or balloon. The horse that pulled the cart would provide an added benefit, with the manure that could be collected and sold to gardeners for a few pennies.
	Religion	Children were taught to behave and respect their elders and never answer back. They were also required to show due reverence towards aunties and uncle, and would be severely scolded for causing trouble to neighbours.
	Respect	Churches, chapels and Sunday schools had a wide impact on Black Country communities for most of the twentieth century, and services were always well attended. Sunday processions, church bells and the Salvation Army were a familiar part of a Sunday. In addition, the numerous church schools had an enormous influence.
S	Smog	A mixture of smoke and fog is a very unpleasant memory of the dangerous industrial pollution that covered the whole region until the Clean Air Act of 1956. This mixture of deadly factory and domestic fire smoke was an ever-present health hazard during the winter months. For anyone with chest complaints or similar problems it could be fatal. In 1952, a particularly bad winter with the added danger of numerous foggy nights, the total fatalities reached a record level.
	Sport	Professional and amateur sport has always been an integral part of Black Country character: football, cricket, rugby, bowls, and horse and greyhound racing in particular. Most local industries provided excellent sporting facilities for their employees. Across the region, amateur leagues attracted a great amount of participation from enthusiastic local people of all ages.

Queuing became a habit

T	Teenagers	A description unknown in Black Country communities up until the mid-fifties. Most boys and girls left school at 14 and started work, moving straight to the status of adult at the age of 21. The concept of 'teenagers' emerged in the fifties and, as the chill of post-war austerity slowly subsided, people's income increased and teenagers were targeted by the business world as a group with money to spend – which they did, on their own fashion styles, records, food, music and cosmetics.
	Television	Initially in the late forties, television was regarded by many people as a gimmick and novelty that would never catch on. The cost of a TV in relation to the average wage was beyond most household incomes. This changed in 1953 with the televising of the coronation. From then on it became a must-have item for every family home and a dominant factor of people's daily lives.
U	Unions	Organised unions have a long history of activity centred on the Black Country region. The area played a major role in campaigning for better working conditions, improved pensions and wages. Also, people from the area battled for a shorter working week.

V	Votes for women	Undoubtedly the huge role that women from this region and elsewhere played in helping to win two world wars greatly influenced the decision to sanction voting rights for women in 1918, in part because of their contribution to ammunition and shell production.
	Voluntary work	Voluntary organisations have a long, proud record throughout the Black Country. Men and women belonging to church groups, tenants and residents' associations, Girl Guides, Boy Scouts, Boys' Brigade and many more voluntary groups, have all contributed time and effort for their communities over many decades.
W	Wartime	The Black Country played a part in both world wars of the twentieth century. Its industries were vital to ensuring ultimate victory, and while the region's men can boast of a proud record of serving in the armed forces, its women took their places on the factory floor and ensured essential wartime productivity was maintained.
	Wireless radio	Between the twenties and the fifties, radio – or the wireless as it was then called – dominated people's leisure hours, until it was overtaken by television in 1953. In the war years it was a crucial contact between the government and the people, and helped to maintain morale throughout the conflict.
X	Xenophobia	The people of the Black Country were often characterised as suspicious of strangers not born in the area.
Y	Yuletide	In the Black Country, the custom of celebrating Christmas and New Year was always a large family occasion, as they gathered to hold house parties and exchange news and events. It was also a time of strong religious involvement with essential attendance at carol and midnight services.
Z	Zeal	The ability, passed down from generation to generation, of Black Country people to overcome all kinds of hardships in their daily lives.
	Zenith	The Black Country at the height of its industrial power as the manufacturing hub of the nation.

Typical Weekly Chores and Household Routine around the First Half of the Twentieth Century

There were certain basic things that would be done every day in a typical household, such as cleaning out ashes and lighting fires, daily shopping and preparing meals, getting the family to bed at night and preparing working clothes and uniforms, and making sandwiches for their lunch boxes.

Sunday	Attending church or chapel	Smartly dressed Shoes polished Sunday school
	Sewing and mending	Threw away nothing Hand sewing Thimbles Rug making
	Visiting relatives and friends	Exchange news Gossip on the street
Monday	Wash day starts at 6.30 a.m.	Clean out boiler Light the fire Heavy physical work Using dolly tub and mangle Recketts blue Fear of rain and bad weather
	Wash down the brew house floor	
Tuesday	Ironing Day	Using heavy irons Checking temperature of iron
	Emptying chamber pots	Washing out with Jeyes Fluid Scrubbing out
Wednesday	Cleaning bedrooms and carpets	Sprinkle water and salt on carpets and brushing in Taking carpets outside, putting on line and beating out dirt
	Cleaning windows	
Thursday	All tiled floors cleaned	Red Cardinal polish
	Baking day	Baking bread Bread pudding from any stale bread Apple pie in season Cakes
Friday	Black leading the grate	Zebra Polish and brushes
	Polishing the brasses	Brasso Polish and rags
	Relief from cooking	Fish & chips for supper, especially for Catholics
	Bath night	Tin bath fetched in Water boiling Who had the first bath? Rota for boys and girls
Saturday	Main shopping day	Visit the main town Late visit to market for bargains
	Cleaning bedrooms	
	Changing bed linen	

All these chores and household duties had to be done without any household gadgets to help them such as:

Washing machines
Dishwashers
Vacuum cleaners
Electric toasters
Refrigerators
Freezers
Electric kettles
Electric fires
Few cookers (just an open fire)

There were also no fitted carpets, central heating or washing up liquid. On top of all this, housewives faced the problem of having to maintain an open fire for cooking, heating the house, and boiling water for shaving and washing. In winter months, with so many families sharing outside toilets and the only tap water being situated in the brew house, there was the constant headache of frozen pipes to contend with. For thousands living in courtyards and back-to-back properties, the summer period meant coping with a total lack of cold food space to protect perishable items. Finally, there was the challenge of running a home, which the vast majority had to do on a pittance of a weekly income that meant they had constantly to scrimp and save from week to week, requiring them to use every penny wisely.

Acknowledgements

Many thanks are due to the people who have assisted me in many ways during the writing of this book: John Workman from *Black Country Bugle*, Ann Ramsbottom, Simon Archer (Editor of Black Country Magazines), Bill Howe, Jim Ramsbottom, Mark F Evans, the members of the Black Country Memories Club and, most importantly, to my wife Emily for all her support and advice.

For those who supplied me with pictures, thanks to: Joan Tranter and family, Megan Fitzgerald Plummer, Jill Brownhill Wildman from History of Bradley and Bilston (Facebook), Ted Garbett, The History of Wednesbury (Facebook), Peter Madley *Express & Star*, John Workman of the *Black Country Bugle* and the staff of Wolverhampton Archives..

Previous Publications by Tom Larkin

Reflections of the Twentieth Century, 1998
Black Country Chronicles, 2009